101
MODEL RAILROAD
LAYOUTS

101
MODEL RAILROAD LAYOUTS

BY PAUL GARRISON

TAB **TAB BOOKS Inc.**
BLUE RIDGE SUMMIT, PA. 17214

FIRST EDITION
FIRST PRINTING

Copyright © 1983 by TAB BOOKS Inc.
Printed in the United States of America

Library of Congress Cataloging in Publication Data

Garrison, Paul.
101 model railroad layouts.

Includes index.
1. Railroads—Models. I. Title. II. Title: One
hundred one model railroad layouts. III. Title: One
hundred and one model railroad layouts.
TF197.G368   1983   625.1'9   82-19375
ISBN 0-8306-0514-2
ISBN 0-8306-1514-8 (pbk.)

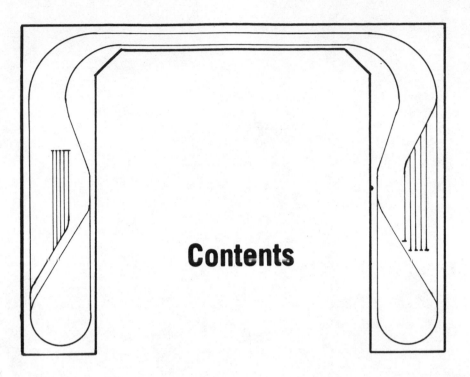

Contents

Other TAB books by the author:

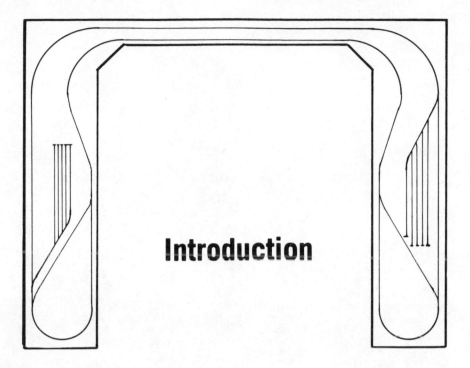

Introduction

This book is divided into six parts. The first part deals with layouts designed primarily to run trains continuously. The layouts start with a simple oval and graduate to fairly complicated track plans.

The second part deals with layouts; the primary purpose is to illustrate point-to-point operation. These are most like the kinds of operations conducted in the real world.

The third part deals with layouts that are best suited to out-and-return operation.

The next part deals with trolley car layouts and layouts combining trolley car operations and railroad operations.

The last part is devoted to layouts that permit a wide variety of different types of operation.

Before you start, always remember that good track work will give long hours of pleasure. Sloppy track work will give much longer hours of aggravation. Now it's time to get started.

Have fun!

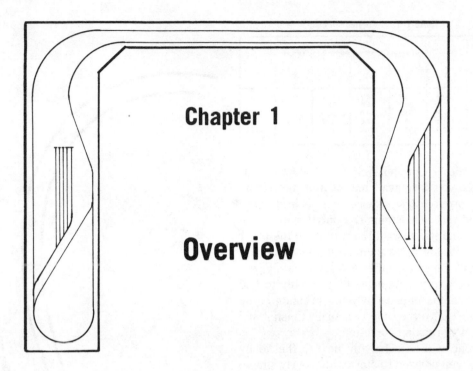

Chapter 1

Overview

The purpose of this book is to act as a thought starter. There is no need to follow to the letter any of the track plans included in the following pages. Pick one or several that appeal to you and then modify them to fit your likes and the space that you happen to have available for your layout.

Each illustration is accompanied by a table of parameters (stating the type of operation for which it was designed), the suggested size of the layout for each of the six popular gauges, the approximate number of feet of track required (not including stations or freight yards), the number of turnouts and crossovers (again excluding stations and yards), the number of actual track crossings (and, in parentheses, the number of overpasses and underpasses), the number of stations or yards, the number of return loops that permit reversal of train travel, and the number of wyes that can be used for the same purpose.

I have also listed the number of scale miles represented by the main line portions of the track, and the time it will take a train to cover that distance at a scale speed of 35 mph.

The term scale speed might need a bit of explanation. The most convenient means of measuring scale speed is by equating it to the number of inches or feet that a train on your layout will travel in one minute. Table 1-1 shows different prototype speeds opposite the number of feet per minute traveled by your model train on your layout. By placing your rheostat on a specific setting and watching a certain engine cover a section of track—the length of which you know—and timing its passage, you can determine the scale speed at which that train is traveling.

Modelers are usually prone to having trains travel much too fast. Therefore, it is a good exercise to learn what true prototype speeds look like when they are translated into scale speeds.

Designing a model railroad layout can be a lot of fun, but it can also be a frustrating experience. Some of the ideas you will fall in love with simply won't work. When you play around with pencil and paper, you will often find that you allow much too little space for curves and loops. After having come up with what you might like to think of as a dream

Table 1-1. Prototype Speeds.

Prototype speed in miles per hour	Scale speeds in feet per minute for six gauges					
	O	S	OO	HO	TT	N
10	20.2	15.2	12.7	11.1	8.1	6.1
20	40.4	30.4	25.4	22.2	16.2	12.2
35	70.7	53.0	44.6	39.0	28.3	21.2
50	101.0	75.8	63.6	55.7	40.4	30.3
100	202.0	151.6	127.2	111.4	80.8	60.6

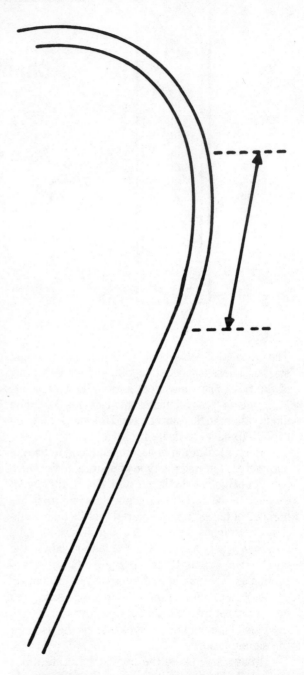

layout, it either can't possibly be fitted into whatever space you have available for it or there is no place to store rolling stock when it is not in use. You might find that your trains can only travel in one direction, and if you want them to go in the other direction, you must pick them up and put them back on the track facing the other way. Alternately, you might plan a very complicated layout only to find that after months, or possibly years, of building, you simply don't have the time to actually finish it and maintain it in running condition.

Anyone who is relatively new to the hobby would be well advised to start with a fairly simple and unambitious design. Finish it and get it to work properly. Once that has been accomplished, it is always an easy matter to extend the original layout if additional space is available.

Two important prerequisites for smooth operation must always be kept in mind. One has to do with the transition from straight track into a curve. The curve should always develop gradually (see Fig. 1-1) because the shock that results when a train, traveling at reasonably high speed, suddenly hits a fairly tight curve will only too often result in derailments. Whenever a curve is planned, leave a little extra room for a section of track to serve as a lead-in to that curve.

The other factor to remember is the length of track needed to achieve a sufficient degree of change in elevation to have one track pass safely over or under another. As a general rule, prototype railroads rarely exceed a 2.5 percent grade (the track rises or drops 2.5 feet in 100 feet). Most model railroaders are nearly always cramped for space and you might have to compromise in this area.

While 2.5 percent is ideal, you can usually get

Fig. 1-1. Always leave room to lead gradually into a curve. This will be a great help in assuring reliable operation without derailments.

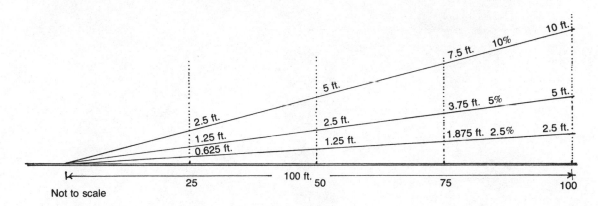

Not to scale

Fig. 1-2. Grades should be kept as shallow as possible, but it takes a lot of track length to achieve the change in elevation necessary to have one train pass over or under the other.

Table 1-2. Inches of Track and Altitude Change.

Gauge	Elevation change in inches	Percent grade (2.5% is ideal)				
		2%	2.5%	3%	4%	5%
0	5″	250″	200″	166.7″	125″	100″
S	3.8″	190″	152″	126.7″	95″	76″
OO	3.1″	155″	124″	103.3″	77.5″	67″
HO	2.8″	140″	112″	93.3″	70″	56″
TT	2.0″	100″	80″	66.7″	50″	40″
N	1.5″	75″	60″	50″	37.5″	30″

away with as much as 5 percent. Some engines might have trouble getting a long train up such an incline. Figure 1-2 is a graphic representation (not to scale) of the relationship between elevation change and length of track.

Table 1-2 shows the number of inches of track that is required in order to achieve the minimum altitude change that is needed to have one train pass safely above or below the other—in each of the six major gauges—at anywhere from 2 to 5 percent grade. This is a handy table to have because it tells you at a glance how much track you must count on in order to allow for an overpass or underpass somewhere down the road.

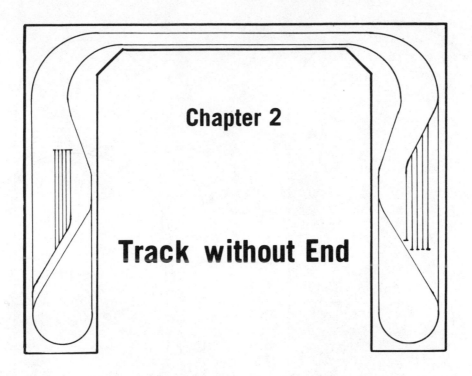

Chapter 2

Track without End

For most of us, the earliest exposure to something resembling model railroading was a box under the Christmas tree containing a brightly colored engine, two or three equally garish cars, and a sufficient number of track sections to construct an oval. On such an oval, you could then run the train, usually at too high a speed, around and around ad infinitum. This unpretentious oval is the basis for some 90 percent of all model railroad layouts, no matter how convoluted they might appear, because it is the oval that permits trains to run continuously without the need for a lot of attention.

This section of the book is devoted primarily to layouts that are designed to permit such continuous operations. This chapter begins with some very simple designs and graduates to the more complex.

Illustration A of Fig. 2-1 is used here simply as a reminder that it is the oval that is at the bottom of all that follows. And B of Fig. 2-1 is an oval twisted like a pretzel to increase the length of time it will take the train to get back to the starting point. There are no turnouts, sidings, or spurs. It is simply one continuous track that runs over and under itself. If this design is built using the sizes indicated, the track will represent 2.03 prototype miles. Traveling at a scale speed of 35 miles per hour, the train, regardless of gauge, will take 3 minutes and 29 seconds to run one complete circuit.

A layout such as this will become rather boring except for those modelers who are really not interested in railroad operations. The train and tracks could be used primarily as an excuse to construct some intricate landscaping with detailed bridges, trestles, and such.

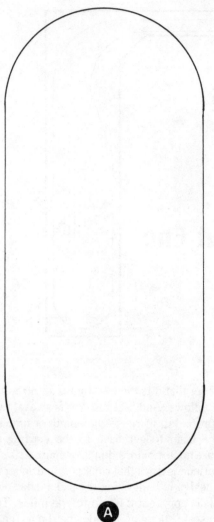

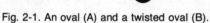

Fig. 2-1. An oval (A) and a twisted oval (B).

LAYOUT 1

While the layouts shown in B of Fig. 2-1 look like three ovals carelessly tossed one on top of the other, they actually are simply one oval twisted around several times to create a longer track in a limited space. It represents a nice beginning for a novice modeler who does not as yet know whether he or she wants to concentrate on train operations or on landscaping. It also helps you learn about elevations, grades, and such. All those tracks have to pass over or under each other.

Type:	Continuous Run	
Gauge	Layout in Feet	Track in Feet
O	43 x 23	247
S	33 x 18	185
OO	27 x 15	155
HO	24 x 13	136
TT	17 x 9	99
N	13 x 7	74

Remarks:
Scale Miles: 2.03
Running Time at 35 mph: 0:03:29

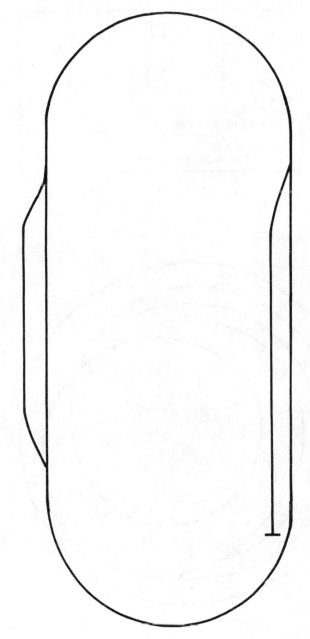

LAYOUT 2

Here we're going one step ahead. Added to the basic oval are a passing siding and a spur. Now you have three turnouts. This requires three switch machines and two switch-machine controls. Now two trains can pass one another, and rolling stock can be stored on the siding when it is not in use.

Type:	Continuous Run	
Gauge	Layout in Feet	Track in Feet
O	27 x 13	77
S	20 x 10	58
OO	17 x 8	48
HO	15 x 7	42
TT	11 x 5	31
N	8 x 4	23

Turnouts
  Left Hand: 1
  Right Hand: 2

Scale Miles: 0.63
Running Time at 35 mph: 0:01:05

LAYOUT 3

For all practical purposes, this is the same layout as the one in the previous layout. It is shown in its basic configuration. At the right is the same layout twisted upon itself to make the track longer and to make the visual aspect of the operation more interesting.

Type:	Continuous Run	
Gauge	Layout in Feet	Track in Feet
O	13 x 13	157
S	10 x 10	118
OO	8 x 8	99
HO	7 x 7	86
TT	5 x 5	63
N	4 x 4	47

Turnouts
  Left Hand: 1 curved
  Right Hand: 2 curved

Scale Miles: 1.29
Running Time at 35 mph: 0:02:13

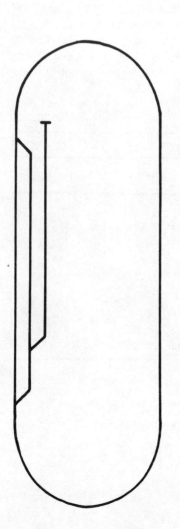

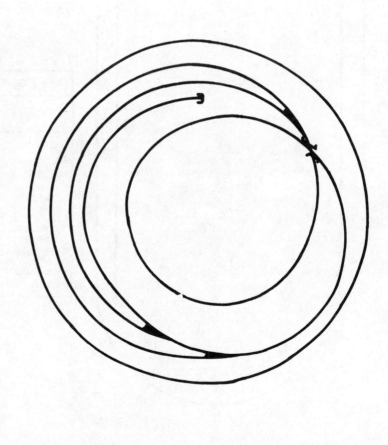

LAYOUT 4

This is another variation on the same theme. Again there is one passing siding and a spur. But there is more track and it will take the train longer to travel over the entire length of the mainline.

Type:	Continuous Run	
Gauge	Layout in Feet	Track in Feet
O	17 x 17	120
S	13 x 13	90
OO	10 x 10	76
HO	9 x 9	66
TT	7 x 7	48
N	5 x 5	36

Turnouts
  Left Hand: 1
  Right Hand: 2
Stations: 1

Scale Miles: 0.99
Running Time at 35 mph: 0:01:42

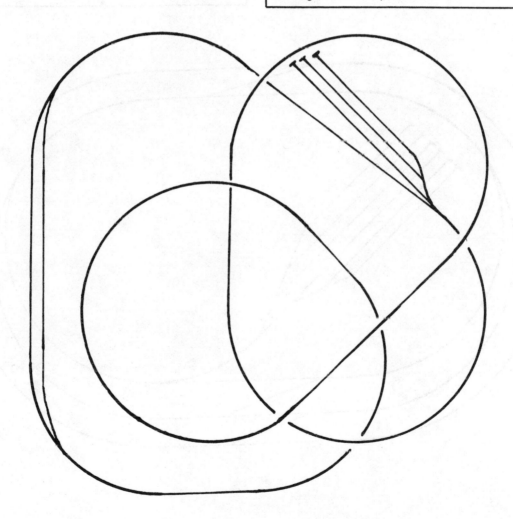

LAYOUT 5

Here I have made things a little more complicated. There are two separate ovals connected by a crossover. Again there is one passing siding and a spur that now has grown into a small station. Because the two ovals can be operated as separate entities, it is now possible to run two trains at the same time.

Type:	Continuous Run	
Gauge	Layout in Feet	Track in Feet
O	20 x 13	113
S	15 x 10	85
OO	13 x 8	71
HO	11 x 7	62
TT	8 x 5	45
N	6 x 4	34

Turnouts
  Right Hand: 1
  Single Crossover: 3
Stations: 1

Scale Miles: 0.93
Running Time at 35 mph: 0:01:36

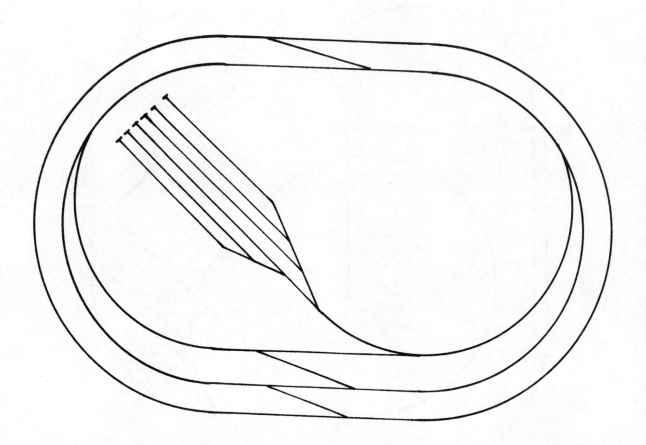

LAYOUT 6

Here is another basic oval with a section of track that can double for a passing siding and a spur. This time I have added two stations so that a train leaving station 1 can run around the main line for a while before finally coming to a stop in station 2 to unload passengers or freight.

Type: Continuous Run		
Gauge	Layout in Feet	Track in Feet
O	20 x 18	100
S	15 x 14	75
OO	13 x 12	63
HO	11 x 10	55
TT	8 x 7	40
N	6 x 5.5	30

Turnouts
  Left Hand: 4
  Right Hand: 1

Stations: 2

Scale Miles: 0.82
Running Time at 35 mph: 0:01:25

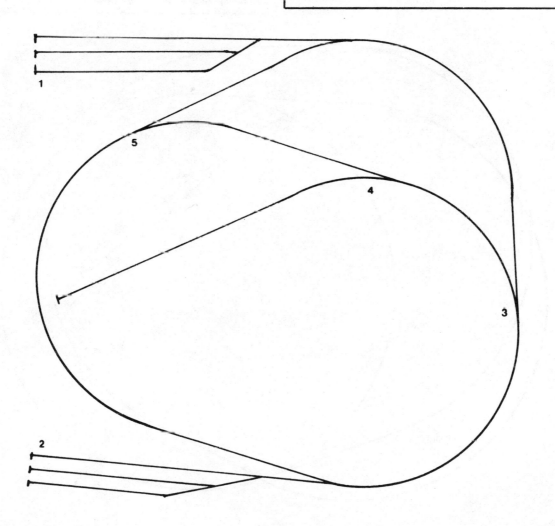

LAYOUT 7

Here we go back to that basic oval with a connecting track that can double as a passing siding. The single tip switch at the left of the illustration adds variety and interest to the operational possibilities of this very simple layout.

Type: Continuous Run		
Gauge	Layout in Feet	Track in Feet
O	22 x 18	107
S	16 x 14	80
OO	14 x 12	67
HO	12 x 10	59
TT	9 x 7	43
N	6.5 x 5.5	32

Turnouts
  Left Hand: 1
  Right Hand: 2

Stations: 1

Scale Miles: 0.88
Running Time at 35 mph: 0:01:30

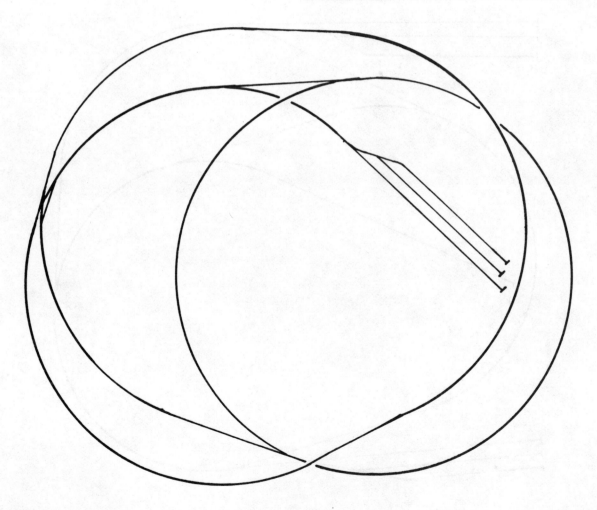

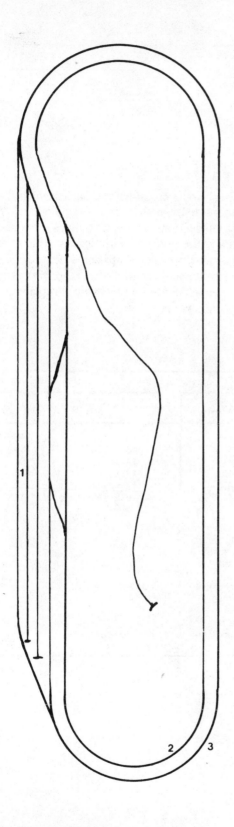

LAYOUT 8

Here are two entirely separate ovals, a station, and a spur. The two separate ovals are connected by two crossovers. The tracks on the far right and left of station 1 can double as passing sidings. A local can hold in the station on one of those tracks while an express goes by on the other. At the same time, a freight could be running continuously on the inner oval.

Type:	Continuous Run	
Gauge	Layout in Feet	Track in Feet
O	30 x 10	183
S	23 x 8	138
OO	19 x 6	115
HO	17 x 5	101
TT	12 x 4	73
N	9 x 3	55

Turnouts
  Left Hand: 2
  Right Hand: 2
  Single Crossover: 2
Stations: 1

Scale Miles: 1.51
Running Time at 35 mph: 0:02:36

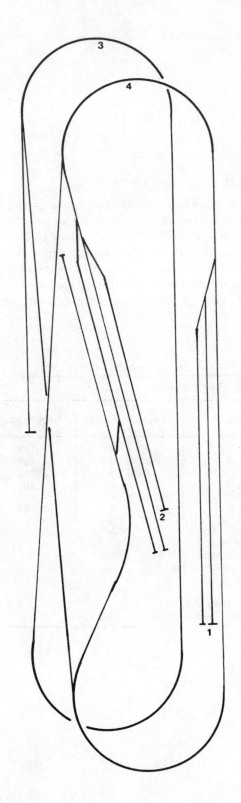

LAYOUT 9

This layout consists of two separate ovals, but that fact is distinguished by overlapping and connecting rail sections. In addition, there is one more station and the possible variations in train operations have been increased to some degree. These variations can be increased even more if the overpass on the left center of the layout is replaced by a double slip switch.

Type: Continuous Run		
Gauge	Layout in Feet	Track in Feet
O	30 x 15	143
S	23 x 11	108
OO	19 x 9	90
HO	17 x 8	79
TT	12 x 6	57
N	9 x 4.5	43

Turnouts
  Left Hand: 1
  Right Hand: 3
  Single Crossover: 1

Crossings: 0 or 2
Stations: 2

Scale Miles: 1.18
Running Time at 35 mph: 0:02:02

LAYOUT 10

This one is kind of tricky. For a moment, try to ignore the two crossovers (3 and 4) and—when trying to follow the run of a train along the tracks—you will find that what we have here are actually two separate continuous-run layouts that are entirely unconnected. This would be ideal if you were building a display, using two different gauges, or if you wanted to operate in the standard and narrow-gauge versions of a given gauge.

On the other hand, if you want to operate in only one gauge the crossovers should be installed. The two separate layouts should be connected to permit the trains to have access to all parts of the trackage.

Type: Continuous Run

Gauge	Layout in Feet	Track in Feet
O	47 x 33	240/183/423
S	35 x 25	180/138/318
OO	29 x 21	151/115/260
HO	26 x 18	132/101/233
TT	19 x 13	96/73/169
N	14 x 10	72/55/127

Turnouts
  Left Hand: 1
  Right Hand: 1
  Single Crossover: 2
Stations: 1

Scale Miles: 1.98/1.51/3.49
Running Time at 35 mph: 0:03:24/0:02:35/0:05:59

Remarks:
This layout consists of two separate track plans connected only by the (optional) crossovers. Data are listed as: Track plan 1/Track plan 2/Combined.

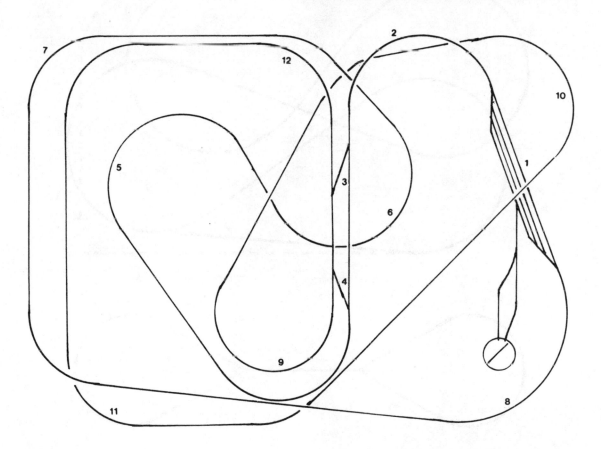

LAYOUT 11

Now we are coming to the subject of providing the operator with an opportunity to reverse the direction of train travel. In the simplified diagram on the left of this layout, there is a straight section of main line ending in two return loops. Because that is somewhat dull, the layout on the right side of the illustration has simply taken that same principle and bent it upon itself. Also indicated by dotted lines are two optional spurs or stations.

Type:	Continuous Run	
Gauge	Layout in Feet	Track in Feet
O	17 x 10	157
S	13 x 8	118
OO	10 x 6	99
HO	9 x 5.5	86
TT	7 x 4	63
N	5 x 3	47

Turnouts
  Right Hand: 2
Crossings: 4 (or overpasses)
Return Loops: 2

Scale Miles: 1.23
Running Time at 35 mph: 0:02:13

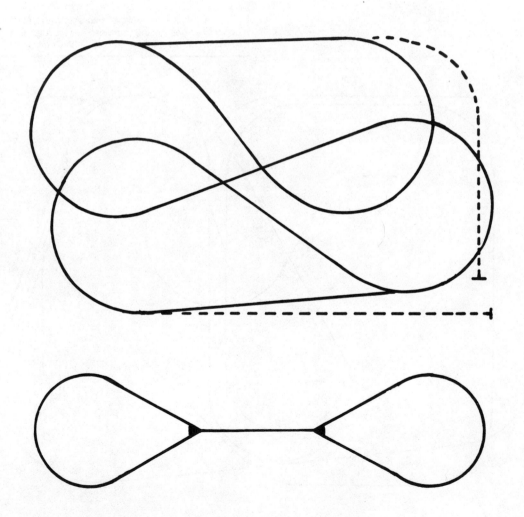

LAYOUT 12

This is basically a figure eight with two connecting sections of track that place the figure eight inside a simple oval. While this might not be much of a layout, it does permit reversal of travel direction or continuous operation in one direction or the other. It is shown here simply because it frequently is the principle on which much more intricate layouts can be designed.

Type:	Continuous Run	
Gauge	Layout in Feet	Track in Feet
O	20 x 13	113
S	15 x 10	85
OO	13 x 8	71
HO	11 x 7	62
TT	8 x 5	45
N	6 x 4	34

Turnouts
  Left Hand: 2
  Right Hand: 2
  Y: 2
Return Loops: 2
Wyes: 2

Scale Miles: 0.93
Running Time at 35 mph: 0:01:36

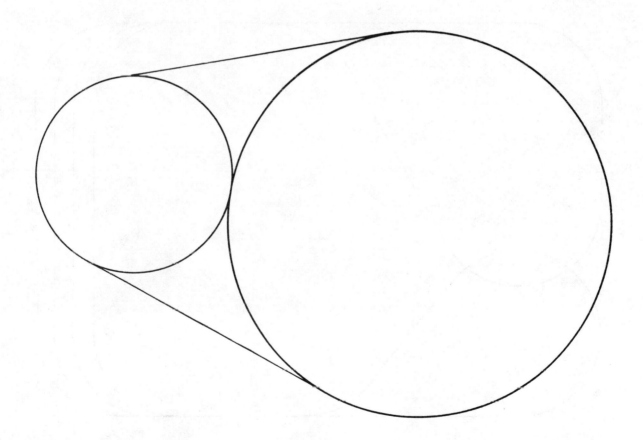

LAYOUT 13

This is another case where two reverse loops are connected by a main line. On that main line you can indicate a group of passing sidings, a station, a freight yard, or whatever appeals to you. It is more of a principle on which a more elaborate layout can be based rather than a complete layout.

Type:	Continuous Run	
Gauge	Layout in Feet	Track in Feet
O	63 x 40	353
S	48 x 30	265
OO	40 x 25	223
HO	35 x 22	195
TT	25 x 16	141
N	19 x 12	106

Turnouts
  Left Hand: 5
  Right Hand: 5
Crossings: 0 (2)
Stations: 1
Return Loops: 2

Scale Miles: 2.91
Running Time at 35 mph: 0:05:00

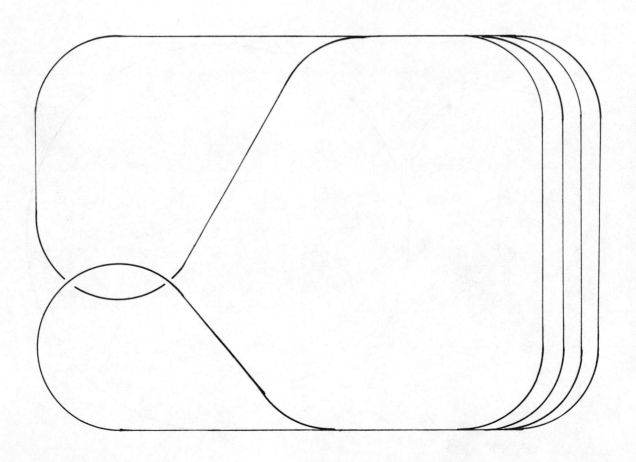

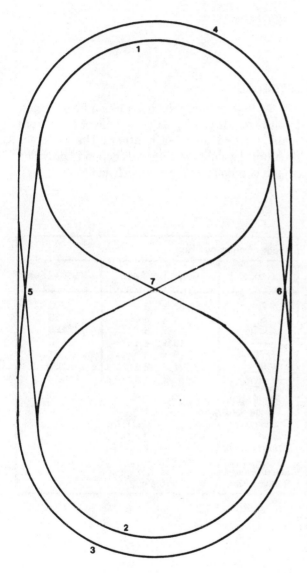

LAYOUT 14

Here is another application of the figure eight. This time it is combined with two interconnected ovals. It requires eight turnouts, two 10-degree track crossings, and one 45-degree crossing. While it is basically a very simple layout, an operator would have his or her hands full running more than one train at a time.

Type: Continuous Run		
Gauge	Layout in Feet	Track in Feet
O	20 x 13	150
S	15 x 10	113
OO	13 x 8	94
HO	11 x 7	83
TT	8 x 5	60
N	6 x 4	45

Turnouts
  Left Hand: 4
  Right Hand: 4
Crossings: 3
Return Loops: 2

Scale Miles: 1.24
Running Time at 35 mph: 0:02:07

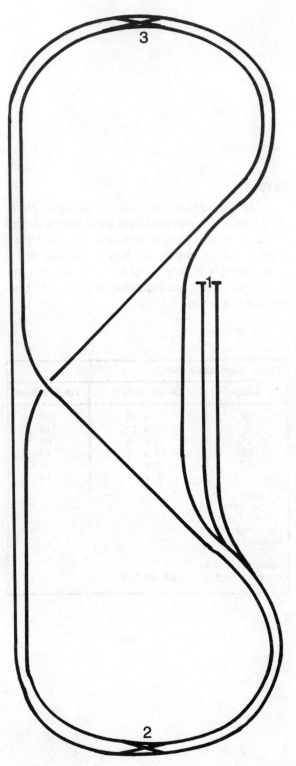

LAYOUT 15

At first glance, this looks like a figure eight, but it is not. It is a layout consisting of two return loops, flipped upon each other. The reverse-direction capability in either direction is provided by the two double crossovers (2 and 3).

Type: Continuous Run		
Gauge	Layout in Feet	Track in Feet
O	23 x 8	203
S	18 x 6	153
OO	15 x 5	128
HO	13 x 4.5	112
TT	9 x 3	81
N	7 x 2.5	61

Turnouts
  Right Hand: 2
  Double Crossover: 2
Crossings: 0 (1)
Stations: 1
Return Loops: 2

Scale Miles: 1.68
Running Time at 35 mph: 0:02:52

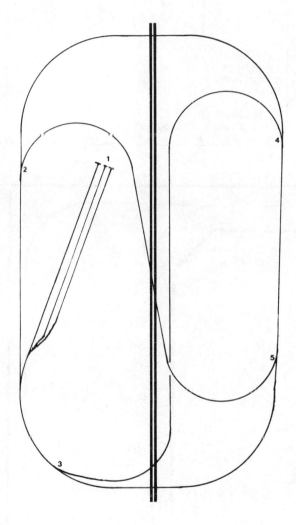

LAYOUT 16

Here we have a simple oval with two return loops. The double lines through the center indicate a background or divider of some kind that separates the layout into two halves. This is strictly a matter of aesthetics. Using such a divider, the layout can be viewed from the right or the left, providing two entirely different views.

Type:	Continuous Run		
Gauge	Layout in Feet		Track in Feet
O	25 x 15		110
S	19 x 11		83
OO	16 x 9		69
HO	14 x 8		61
TT	10 x 6		44
N	7.5 x 4.5		33

Turnouts
  Left Hand: 2
  Right Hand: 2
Crossings: 0 (1)
Stations: 1
Return Loops: 2

Scale Miles: 0.91
Running Time at 35 mph: 0:01:33

Remarks:
  This layout is divided in the center by a background or a high mountain to create two differing environments.

LAYOUT 17

This is a horseshoe-shaped application of the two-return loop (Fig. 2-2). Two track sections can be used for continuous running or as passing sidings. There are several layouts in this book that are versions of this basic design.

Type:	Continuous Run	
Gauge	Layout in Feet	Track in Feet
O	23 x 17	107
S	18 x 13	80
OO	15 x 10	67
HO	13 x 9	59
TT	9 x 7	43
N	7 x 5	32

Turnouts
  Left Hand: 3
  Right Hand: 3
Return Loops: 2

Scale Miles: 0.88
Running Time at 35 mph: 0:01:30

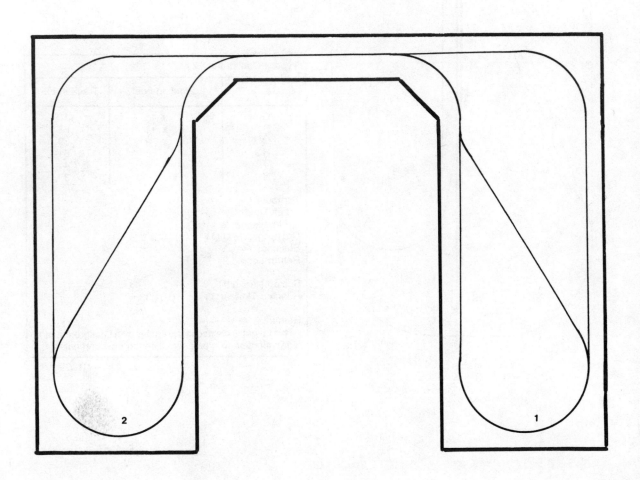

Fig. 2-2. A section of a layout under construction.

LAYOUT 18

Now we're going to get started on some real layouts. This one is oddly shaped in order to allow for furnaces or other obstructions in a basement. It consists of one station, a relatively long main line, and two return loops built into that main line. Depending on the direction of train travel and the way in which turnouts 2 and 3 are set, loop 4 permits the train to reverse direction no matter the direction of travel when entering loop 4.

Type:	Continuous Run	
Gauge	Layout in Feet	Track in Feet
O	50 x 33	170
S	38 x 25	128
OO	31 x 21	107
HO	28 x 18	94
TT	20 x 13	68
N	15 x 10	51

Turnouts
  Left Hand: 2
  Right Hand: 3
Crossings: 1
Stations: 1
Return Loops: 2

Scale Miles: 1.4
Running Time at 35 mph: 0:02:24

LAYOUT 19

This track plan includes one station and two return loops. It is simply a slightly different approach to the same basic principle.

Type: Continuous Run		
Gauge	Layout in Feet	Track in Feet
O	23 x 17	237
S	17.5 x 12.5	178
OO	15 x 10.5	149
HO	13 x 9	130
TT	9 x 7	95
N	7 x 5	71

Turnouts
  Left Hand: 4 (1 curved)
  Right Hand: 5 (1 curved)
Crossings: 0 (2)
Stations: 1
Return Loops: 2
Wyes: 1

Scale Miles: 1.95
Running Time at 35 mph: 0:03:21

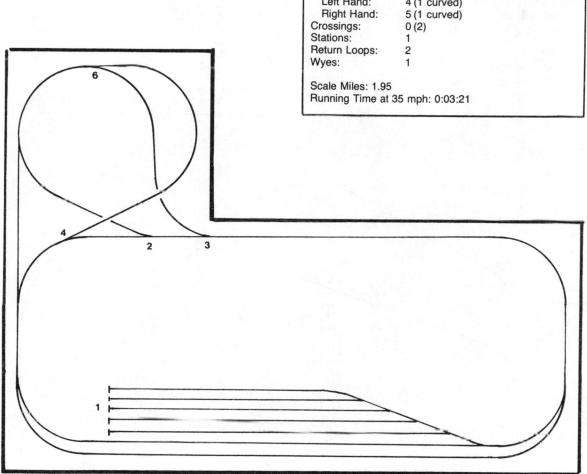

LAYOUT 20

Here is one station, a long main line that includes one return loop, and one wye. A train leaving the station and moving straight through turnout 3 and through the part marked 7 will eventually arrive at turnout 5. If it turns right, it will return to the turnout 3 traveling in the same direction as when it left the station. If it turns left at turnout 5, it will go through turnout 4 and return to turnout 3 heading back toward the station.

After making a left turn at turnout 5, the train cannot again reverse direction unless you take advantage of the wye consisting of turnouts 4, 5, and 6. The train can turn left through turnouts 6 and 5. It will then go back up through turnouts 5 and 4 and move forward through turnouts 4 and 6, having, by this time, reversed its direction of travel.

Type:	Continuous Run	
Gauge	Layout in Feet	Track in Feet
O	23 x 17	150
S	18 x 13	113
OO	15 x 10	94
HO	13 x 9	83
TT	9 x 7	60
N	7 x 5	45

Turnouts
Left Hand: 3
Right Hand: 4
Three Way: 1
Crossings: 0 (4)
Stations: 1
Return Loops: 1
Wyes: 1

Scale Miles: 1.24
Running Time at 35 mph: 0:02:07

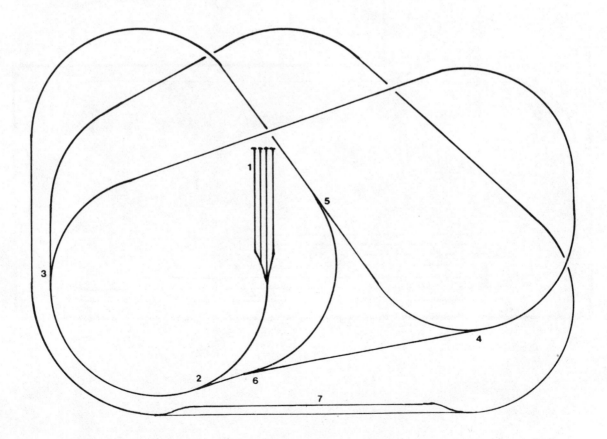

LAYOUT 21

With this layout, a train leaving the station, and moving through turnouts 2, 3, 4, 5, 6, and 7, has the choice of going through 8, 4, and 5 and then turning left to get back to turnout 2 in the same direction of travel as before. Or, once at turnout 7, it can continue on straight and eventually return to the station in the opposite direction.

Simply put, the layout consists of a main line made up of two return loops, plus, of course, the station or storage tracks.

Type:	Continuous Run	
Gauge	Layout in Feet	Track in Feet
O	27 x 17	93
S	20 x 12.5	70
OO	17 x 10.5	59
HO	15 x 9	51
TT	11 x 7	37
N	8 x 5	28

Turnouts
 Left Hand: 3
 Right Hand: 6
Crossings: 0 (6)
Stations: 1
Return Loops: 2

Scale Miles: 0.77
Running Time at 35 mph: 0:01:19

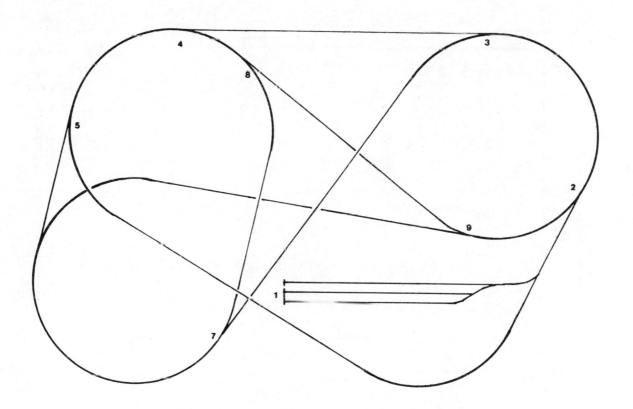

LAYOUT 22

Here is a continuous-run layout designed for a narrow shelf that goes all around the walls of a room. In practice, one section would have to be hinged or removable in order to permit the door to the room to be opened. A layout like this can make use of one shelf of a long bookcase, run along windowsills and such, and thus take up very little room when space is at a premium.

Type: Continuous Run		
Gauge	Layout in Feet	Track in Feet
O	57 x 37	237
S	43 x 28	178
OO	36 x 23	149
HO	31 x 20	130
TT	23 x 15	95
N	17 x 11	71

Turnouts
  Left Hand: 3
  Right Hand: 6
Stations: 3

Scale Miles: 1.95
Running Time at 35 mph: 0:03:21

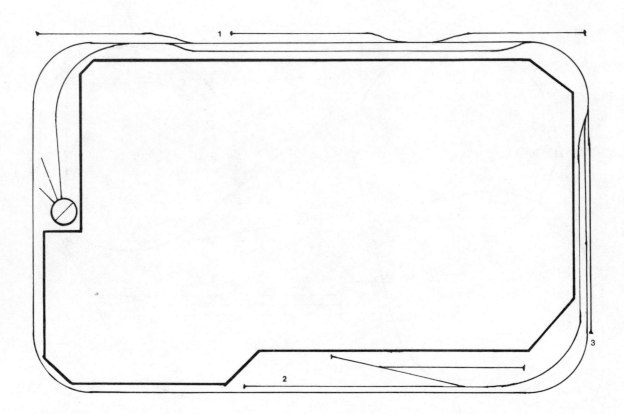

LAYOUT 23

This is an around-the-wall layout that is designed on the same principle as the previous one. The only major difference is the incorporation of a circular space—possibly a coffee table—to add a degree of operational variety.

Type: Continuous Run		
Gauge	Layout in Feet	Track in Feet
O	50 x 33	420
S	38 x 25	315
OO	31 x 21	265
HO	28 x 18	231
TT	20 x 13	168
N	15 x 10	126

Turnouts
  Left Hand: 4
  Right Hand: 4
  Single Crossover: 1
Crossings: 0 (4)
Stations: 2

Scale Miles: 3.46
Running Time at 35 mph: 0:05:56

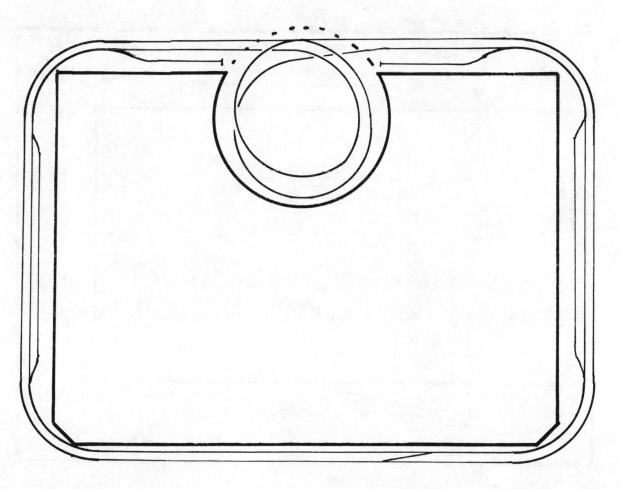

LAYOUT 24

Here is a third variation on the same theme. I have widened the shelf space somewhat to make room for spurs, a yard or station, and a bit more opportunity for landscaping. At point 3, there is a hinged or removable section to facilitate entrance to and exit from the room. If another foot or two of space could be used in one of the upper corners, then it might be possible to add a return loop.

Type:	Continuous Run	
Gauge	Layout in Feet	Track in Feet
O	50 x 37	297
S	38 x 28	223
OO	31 x 23	187
HO	28 x 20	163
TT	20 x 15	119
N	15 x 11	89

Turnouts
  Left Hand: 6
  Right Hand: 6
Crossings: 0 (1)
Stations: 1

Scale Miles: 2.45
Running Time at 35 mph: 0:04:12

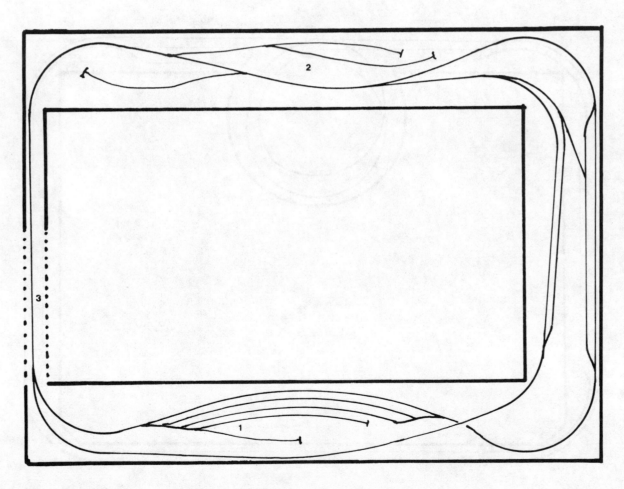

LAYOUT 25

This two-station layout is designed for a limited amount of space. It consists primarily of two separate ovals—permitting the continuous running of two trains—plus the tracks in the center with one through-traffic station and one dead-end station. Depending on the track design in the stations or yards, a fair amount of switching could be added to the continuous-run operations.

Type:	Continuous Run	
Gauge	Layout in Feet	Track in Feet
O	20 x 18	143
S	15 x 14	108
OO	13 x 12	90
HO	11 x 10	79
TT	8 x 7	57
N	6 x 5.5	43

Turnouts
  Left Hand: 2
  Right Hand: 2
  Three Way: 1
Crossings: 2
Stations: 2

Scale Miles: 1.18
Running Time at 35 mph: 0:02:02

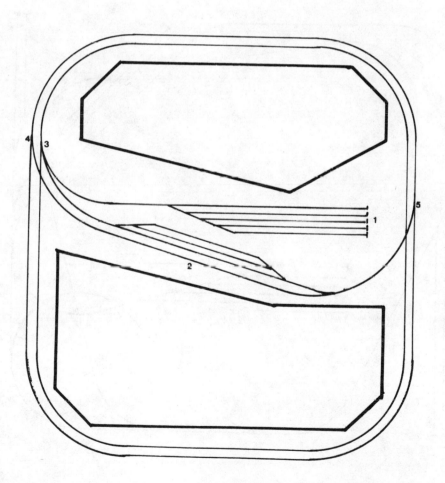

LAYOUT 26

Here is a more extensive layout incorporating four stations or yards (1, 2, 3, and 4), a fair amount of main line, and one return loop (5). This layout also can be squeezed into some fairly small spaces without calling for radii that would be too tight to accommodate long engines or cars.

Type: Continuous Run		
Gauge	Layout in Feet	Track in Feet
O	20 x 18	110
S	15 x 14	83
OO	13 x 12	69
HO	11 x 10	61
TT	8 x 7	44
N	6 x 5.5	33

Turnouts
  Left Hand: 7
  Right Hand: 2
Crossings: 0 (9)
Stations: 4
Return Loops: 1

Scale Miles: 0.91
Running Time at 35 mph: 0:01:33

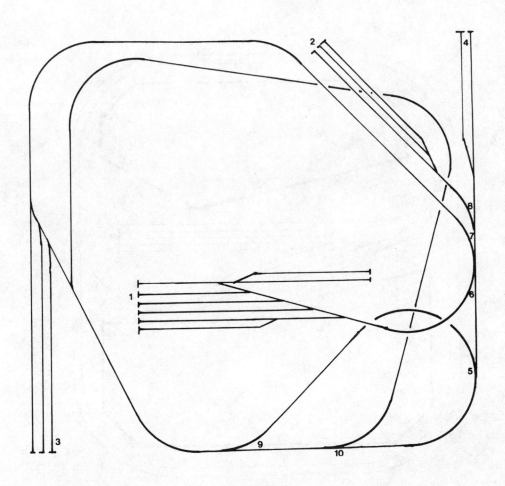

LAYOUT 27

This odd-shaped contraption might be the result of a variety of immovable obstructions in a basement or garage. As is often the case, such unavoidable restrictions to the available space can be the spark that results in interesting track plans. Here is one terminal-type station, one two-track spur, and a lot of convoluted main line. If it were not for the double crossover (4), the only means of having trains reverse direction would be the wye at point 3. By inserting the double crossover, the main line automatically becomes a portion of two return loops.

Type: Continuous Run		
Gauge	Layout in Feet	Track in Feet
O	30 x 20	140
S	23 x 15	105
OO	19 x 13	88
HO	17 x 11	77
TT	12 x 8	56
N	9 x 6	42

Turnouts
  Left Hand: 7
  Right Hand: 5
Crossings: 1 (+2)
Stations: 2
Return Loops: 0 (2)
Wyes: 1

Scale Miles 1.15
Running Time at 35 mph: 0:01:59

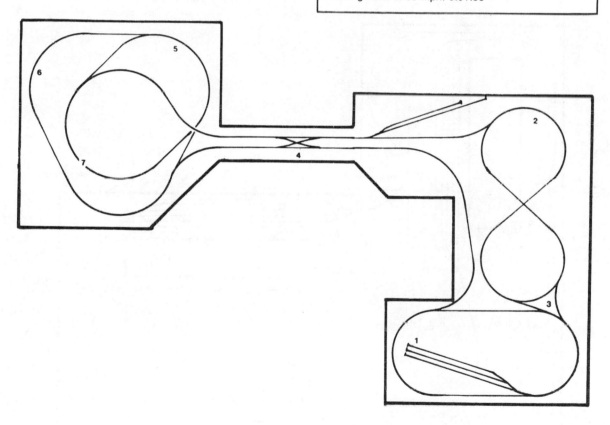

LAYOUT 28

Here is a continuous-run layout that, because of the two passing sidings and the multitrack-through traffic station, could easily be used to run two or even three trains simultaneously. Despite all those curves that look like loops, there is no return loop. If such a loop is preferred, there are two locations at which the addition of two turnouts and a short section of track would accomplish that. One such location is the curve marked 4.

Running a section of track from there to the straight track that leads into curve 5 would transform loop 6 into a return loop. The other location is near station 1. If you run a track from the bottom track of that station to the inner loop curving around the station, you would create a means of reversing the direction of travel.

Type:	Continuous Run	
Gauge	Layout in Feet	Track in Feet
O	25 x 22	187
S	19 x 16	140
OO	16 x 14	118
HO	14 x 12	103
TT	10 x 9	75
N	7.5 x 6.5	56

Turnouts
Left Hand: 4
Right Hand: 3
Crossings: 0 (3)
Stations: 2

Scale Miles: 1.54
Running Time at 35 mph: 0:02:38

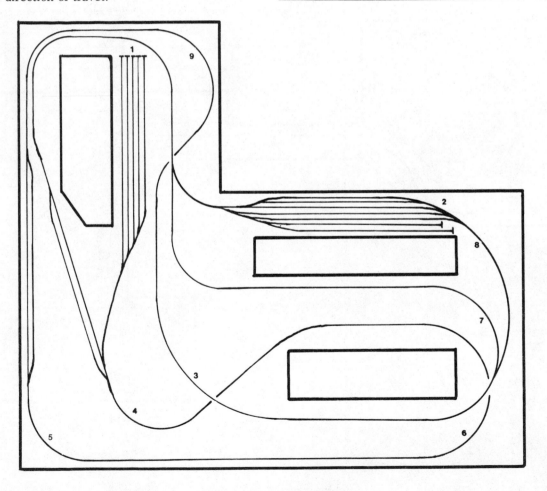

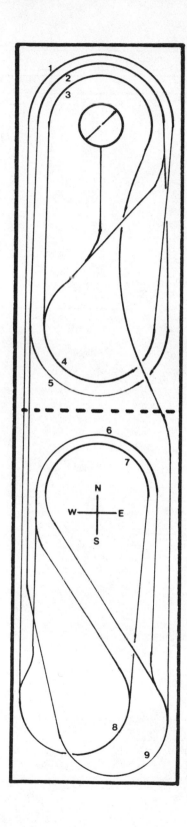

LAYOUT 29

This is a layout that started out originally as a layout just half its size. I built the bottom half (in N gauge) in an apartment in New York. Then, being dissatisfied with the limits to the operation, I added another portion of identical size. By the time all was finished (as finished as a layout ever gets) and connected, I had, at times, four trains running at the same time.

Type:	Continuous Run	
Gauge	Layout in Feet	Track in Feet
O	43 x 8	223
S	33 x 6	168
OO	27 x 5	141
HO	24 x 4.5	123
TT	17 x 3.5	89
N	13 x 2.5	67

Turnouts
   Left Hand: 4
  Right Hand: 3
Crossings: 0 (3)
Stations: 1
Return Loops: 2

Scale Miles: 1.84
Running Time at 35 mph: 0:03:09

LAYOUT 30

This is another of the odd shapes. Here one end is used for a station or yard, plus one return loop, and the rest of the expanse accommodates the main line. A portion, assuming that the various turnouts are properly aligned, can also double as a return loop.

Type:	Continuous Run	
Gauge	Layout in Feet	Track in Feet
O	57 x 33	270
S	43 x 25	203
OO	36 x 21	170
HO	31 x 18	149
TT	23 x 13	108
N	17 x 10	81

Turnouts
Left Hand: 4
Right Hand   1
Single Crossover 1
Crossings: 0 (3)
Stations: 1
Return Loops: 2

Scale Miles: 2.23
Running Time at 35 mph: 0:03:49

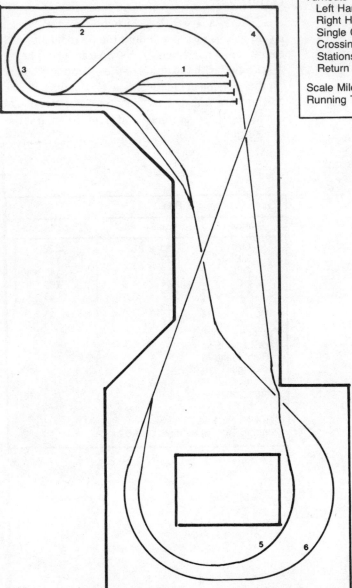

LAYOUT 31

While there is no particular reason to strive for symmetry when it comes to designing a track plan, under certain conditions the available space seems to invite it. Here there are two return loops, two main lines, and two stations. Even though the plan is quite simple, it does allow for quite a bit of operational variety.

Type: Continuous Run		
Gauge	Layout in Feet	Track in Feet
O	57 x 43	287
S	43 x 33	215
OO	36 x 27	181
HO	31 x 24	158
TT	23 x 17	115
N	17 x 13	86

Turnouts
  Left Hand: 2
  Right Hand: 4
Stations: 2
Return Loops: 2

Scale Miles: 2.36
Running Time at 35 mph: 0:04:03

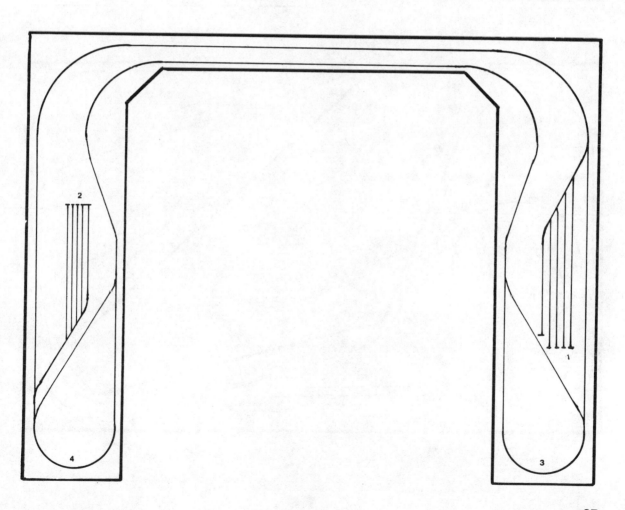

LAYOUT 32

Two stations, a lot of main line that could be running through valleys, along rivers, through tunnels in the mountains, and such—plus one return loop—make up this distorted version of a horseshoe-shaped layout. Actually there are two return loops (3 and 4), but because both serve trains traveling in a specific direction they might just as well be thought of as one.

Type:	Continuous Run	
Gauge	Layout in Feet	Track in Feet
O	53 x 33	327
S	40 x 25	245
OO	34 x 21	206
HO	29 x 18	180
TT	21 x 13	131
N	16 x 10	98

Turnouts
  Left Hand: 3
  Right Hand: 3
  Y: 1
Crossings: 0 (4)
Stations: 2
Return Loops: 1

Scale Miles: 2.69
Running Time at 35 mph: 0:04:37

LAYOUT 33

This layout includes space for some multitrack stations or yards. In addition, there are two main lines (in the area marked 3) that share a common passing siding. While this might seem impractical, it does provide a degree of extra excitement when several trains are being operated at the same time. No provision has been made for a return loop. If such is preferred, a section of track connecting the track marked 7 with the inner track at point 3 would accomplish it.

Type:	Continuous Run	
Gauge	Layout in Feet	Track in Feet
O	30 x 20	310
S	23 x 15	233
OO	19 x 13	195
HO	17 x 11	171
TT	12 x 8	124
N	9 x 6	93

Turnouts
  Left Hand: 6
  Right Hand: 4
Stations: 2

Scale Miles: 2.56
Running Time at 35 mph: 0:04:23

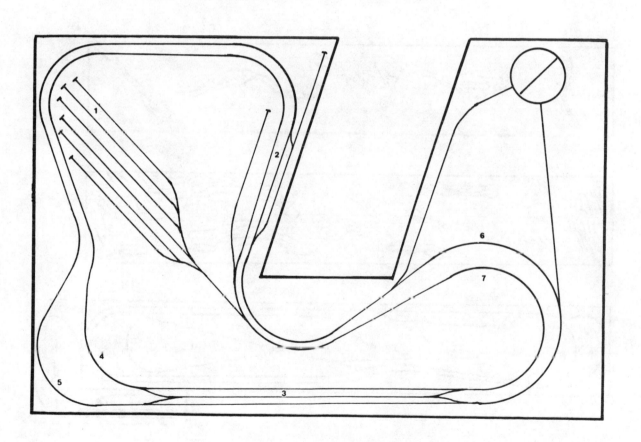

LAYOUT 34

As a general rule, modelers tend to build layouts first and then design the landscaping to fit them. Here the first step was to design a riverbed. The next step called for creating a mountainous landscape through which the river would "flow" and through which the railroad would have to wind its way. See Figs. 2-3, 2-4, and 2-5.

With all that planned, though not necessarily actually built, the track plan was designed. This is an actual layout I once built and operated. After a while, I found that I needed space for a station and yard or, at least, tracks on which to store rolling stock. At that point, I added the section at the top (outlined by the dashed line).

Type:	Continuous Run	
Gauge	Layout in Feet	Track in Feet
O	57 x 10	340
S	43 x 8	225
OO	36 x 6	214
HO	31 x 5.5	187
TT	23 x 4	136
N	17 x 3	102

Turnouts
  Left Hand: 4
  Right Hand: 5
Crossings: 0 (2)
Stations: 1
Return Loops: 2

Scale Miles: 2.8
Running Time at 35 mph: 0:04:48

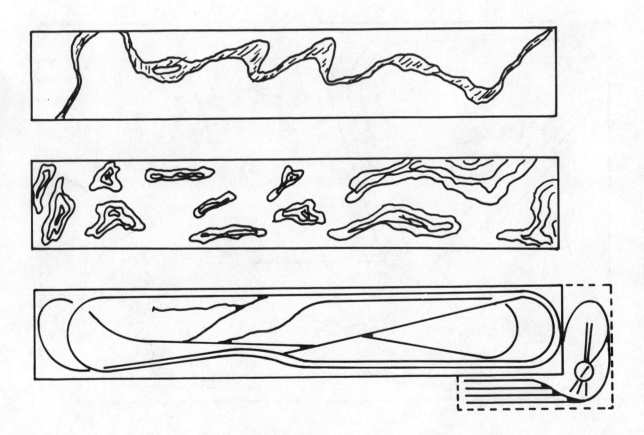

Fig. 2-3. One end of the layout. Note the river in the canyon between the mountains.

Fig. 2-4. By cutting a hole into the end of the layout, a track is laid to a station and yard area that has been added as an afterthought.

Fig. 2-5. One part of the newly added station and yard section is nearly completed.

LAYOUT 35

Here are three ovals. One doubles as a return loop while also sharing a portion of its track with one of the other two ovals. Inside the ovals on the upper right are either one or two stations. The diagonal connecting section of track turns a portion of the inner oval into another return loop. This plan allows for considerable operational variety. This is especially true if more than one train is being operated at the same time.

Type:	Continuous Run	
Gauge	Layout in Feet	Track in Feet
O	53 x 33	343
S	40 x 25	258
OO	34 x 21	216
HO	29 x 18	189
TT	21 x 13	137
N	16 x 10	103

Turnouts
    Left Hand: 2
    Right Hand: 3
    Y: 1
    Single Crossover: 3
Crossings: 1
Stations: 2
Return Loops: 2

Scale Miles: 2.83
Running Time at 35 mph: 0:04:51

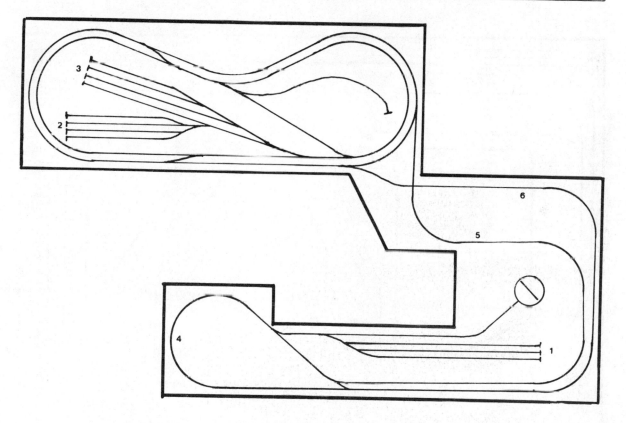

LAYOUT 36

This plan incorporates four stations, two return loops, and enough main-line connections to provide a plethora of complications. This is especially true if a single operator wants to run two or three trains at once. Ideally, this layout would lend itself to scheduled runs between stations, using some local trains that stop everywhere, an express that only stops at, say, two of the stations, plus a lumbering, nonstop freight train.

Type:	Continuous Run	
Gauge	Layout in Feet	Track in Feet
O	57 x 40	347
S	43 x 30	260
OO	36 x 25	218
HO	31 x 22	191
TT	23 x 16	139
N	17 x 12	104

Turnouts
  Left Hand: 8
  Right Hand: 5
  Single Crossover: 4
Crossings: 0 (3)
Stations: 4
Return Loops: 2

Scale Miles: 2.86
Running Time at 35 mph: 0:04:54

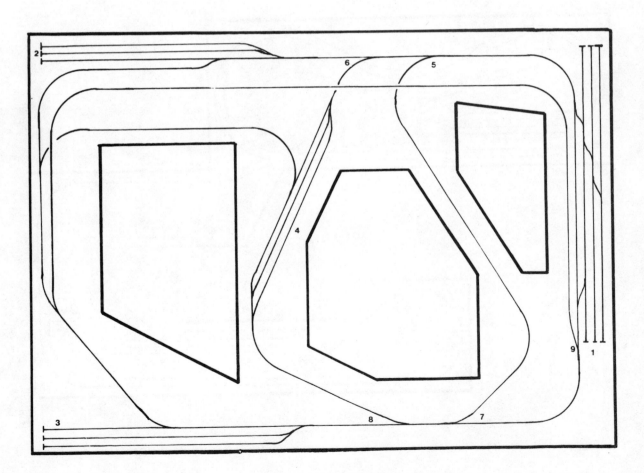

LAYOUT 37

If this layout is built to specifications, it will call for rather tight curves. Operations will be restricted to short engines and cars. If more space is available, then curve radii can be increased and all types of rolling stock can be used.

The layout consists of three stations or yards and quite a bit of main line, portions of which constitute return loops. With two long passing sidings—one along the east side of the layout, the other along the curve that winds around stations 2 and 3—it would be interesting to operate several trains simultaneously.

Type:	Continuous Run	
Gauge	Layout in Feet	Track in Feet
O	28 x 20	210
S	21 x 15	158
OO	18 x 13	132
HO	16 x 11	116
TT	11 x 8	84
N	8.5 x 6	63

Turnouts
  Left Hand: 3
  Right Hand: 5
Crossings: 0 (4)
Stations: 3
Return Loops: 2

Scale Miles: 1.73
Running Time at 35 mph: 0.02.98

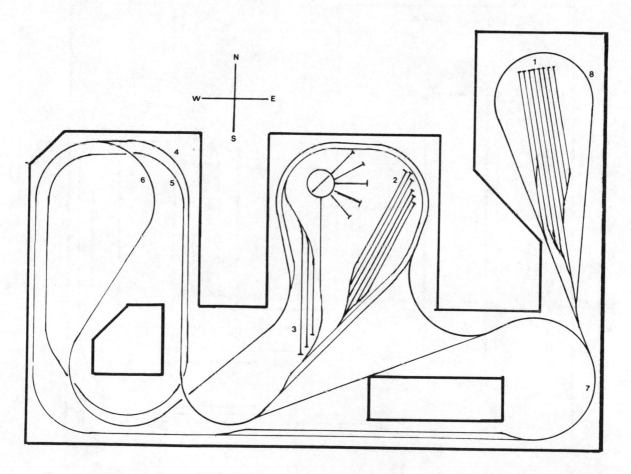

LAYOUT 38

One station, one two-track spur, and a lot of main line make for long, continuous runs. While originally there was no provision for reversal of the direction of train travel, adding the two crossovers at point 3 automatically creates two return loops. This gives the operator complete control over the direction of travel of one or more trains.

Type: Continuous Run		
Gauge	Layout in Feet	Track in Feet
O	50 x 43	393
S	38 x 33	295
OO	31 x 27	248
HO	28 x 24	217
TT	20 x 17	157
N	15 x 13	118

Turnouts
  Left Hand: 2
  Single Crossover: 2
Crossings: 0 (7)
Stations: 2
Return Loops: 2

Scale Miles: 3.24
Running Time at 35 mph: 0:05:34

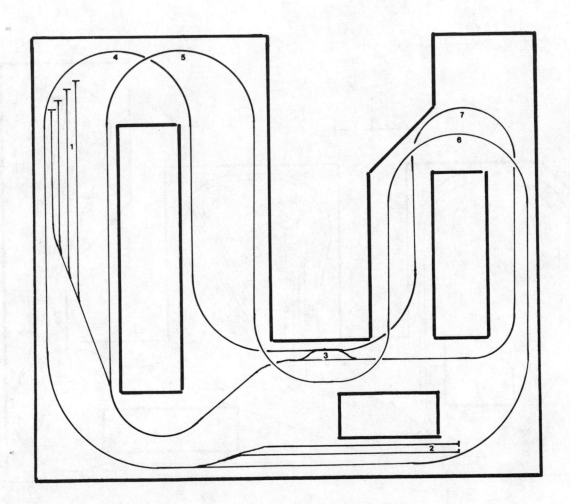

LAYOUT 39

I like this one. If I had the room I'd probably build it. What appeals to me is that there is sufficient main line cramped into a reasonably small space to keep a train running for a long time without constantly retracing its steps.

As the track plan is shown, no provision has been made to reverse the direction of train travel. I would probably try to remedy that, but exactly where would depend on the different levels and elevations of the individual tracks that might make it difficult to connect two without necessitating a much too steep grade.

Type:	Continuous Run	
Gauge	Layout in Feet	Track in Feet
O	50 x 37	443
S	38 x 28	333
OO	31 x 23	279
HO	28 x 20	244
TT	20 x 15	177
N	15 x 11	133

Turnouts
  Left Hand: 4
  Right Hand: 2
Crossings: 0 (12)
Stations: 2

Scale Miles: 3.66
Running Time at 35 mph: 0:06:16

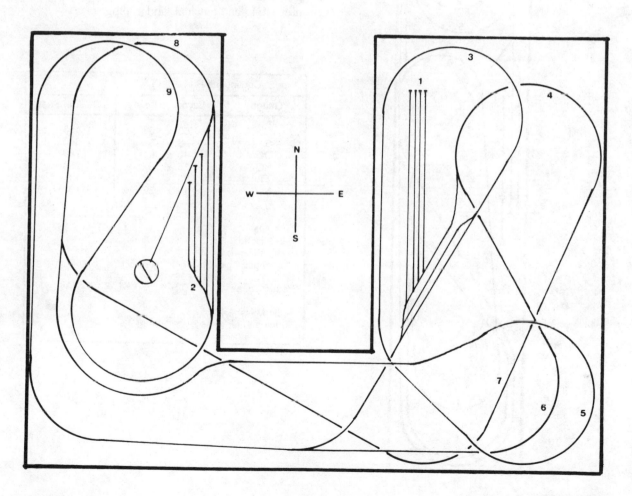

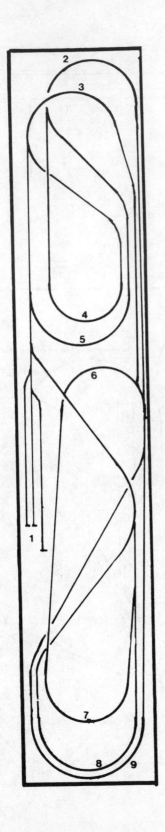

LAYOUT 40

This long and narrow layout accommodates an awful lot of interesting operational opportunities—despite its size. It could be built along the wall of a living room or den or along the backwall of a garage. With the one station, miles of main line and two return loops, you could easily operate two or three trains at a time. Because the layout is as narrow as it is, there are special opportunities for interesting and unusual landscaping.

Type:	Continuous Run	
Gauge	Layout in Feet	Track in Feet
O	63 x 10	453
S	48 x 8	340
OO	40 x 6	286
HO	35 x 5.5	250
TT	25 x 4	181
N	19 x 3	136

Turnouts
  Left Hand: 5
  Right Hand: 2
Crossings: 0 (3)
Stations: 1
Return Loops: 2

Scale Miles: 3.74
Running Time at 35 mph: 0:06:25

LAYOUT 41

This layout has one station along with miles of main line. The whole thing has been fitted into a triangular space. Even though a glance would give the impression that the track plan includes several return loops, this actually is not the case. No provision has been made to reverse direction of travel. Such a provision could, of course, be added at your discretion.

Type:	Continuous Run	
Gauge	Layout in Feet	Track in Feet
O	83 x 57	590
S	63 x 43	443
OO	52 x 36	372
HO	46 x 31	325
TT	33 x 23	236
N	25 x 17	177

Turnouts
  Left Hand: 1
  Right Hand: 4
Crossings: 0 (4)
Stations: 1

Scale Miles: 4.87
Running Time at 35 mph: 0:08:21

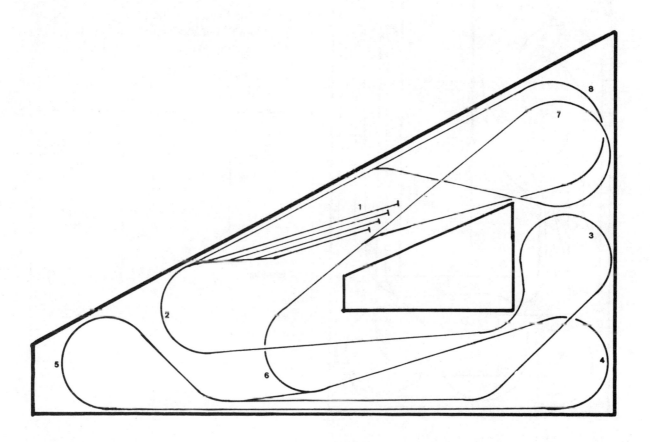

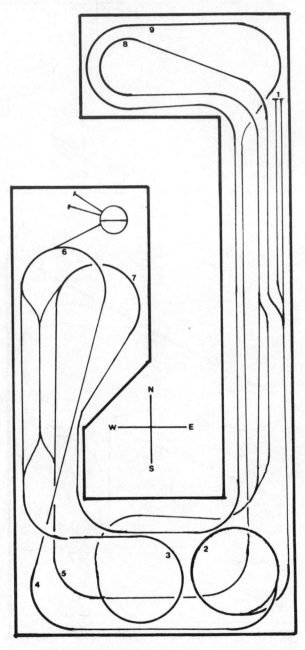

LAYOUT 42

This should really be a big one. If built within the dimensions indicated, a train would be able to travel close to a quarter of an hour (at 35-mph-scale speed) without having to retrace its steps to any great degree. Except for the two-track spur (1), no provision for a station has been made because this is truly a continuous-run layout.

Despite all those loops upon loops, there is no return loop. Such a loop could be added by connecting the inbound and outbound tracks of loop 7 or loop 8 (or both), but this would be something that the builder of the layout would have to decide.

Type: Continuous Run		
Gauge	Layout in Feet	Track in Feet
O	120 x 53	1,040
S	90 x 40	780
OO	76 x 34	655
HO	66 x 29	573
TT	48 x 21	416
N	36 x 16	312

Turnouts
  Left Hand: 6
  Right Hand: 3
  Y: 2
Crossings: 0 (14)
Stations: 2

Scale Miles: 8.58
Running Time at 35 mph: 0:14:42

LAYOUT 43

This is another big one. This time I have added four stations to permit point-to-point operations in addition to continuous runs. While the layout as a whole consists actually of some four interlocked ovals, the curved tracks (marked 5 and 6) are there for the purpose of creating two opposing return loops.

Type: Continuous Run		
Gauge	Layout in Feet	Track in Feet
O	107 x 53	1,113
S	80 x 40	835
OO	67 x 34	701
HO	59 x 29	614
TT	43 x 21	445
N	32 x 16	334

Turnouts
  Left Hand: 6
  Right Hand: 8
Crossings: 2 (+4)
Stations: 4
Return Loops: 2

Scale Miles: 9.18
Running Time at 35 mph: 0:15:44

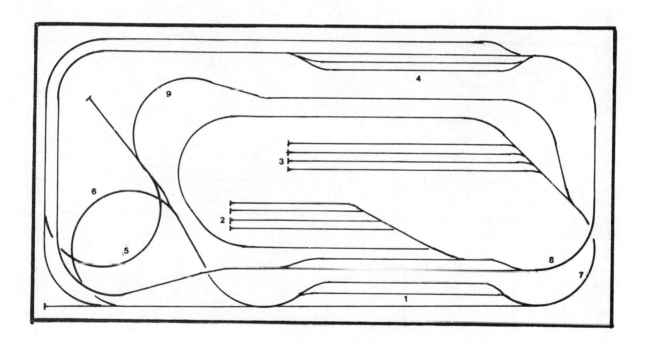

LAYOUT 44

Assuming that the indicated dimensions are used, this is the largest one in the group. It provides for very long, continuous runs. Included in the main line sections are three return loops. These permit trains to change direction of travel at will. Only one station or yard is included (1). It is primarily used for storing rolling stock. This layout is really designed primarily for two or more trains running continuously.

Type:	Continuous Run	
Gauge	Layout in Feet	Track in Feet
O	113 x 73	1,247
S	85 x 55	935
OO	71 x 46	785
HO	62 x 40	687
TT	45 x 29	498
N	34 x 22	374

Turnouts
  Left Hand: 2
  Right Hand: 5
Crossings: 0 (7)
Stations: 1
Return Loops: 3

Scale Miles: 10.28
Running Time at 35 mph: 0:17:38

LAYOUT 45

Here is a track plan for an ambitious modeler with plenty of room at his disposal. In small gauges, it might just fit into a two-car garage. In the larger ones, an entire basement might be required. The basic idea behind the layout is the continuous operation of several trains simultaneously while requiring a minimum of switching.

Let's assume that a train stands ready to go on one of the tracks in station 1, facing south. As it moves out of the station, it passes underneath loop 9 and continues north, and then south until it reaches station 2 where another train may be waiting on the passing siding.

The train continues north and then west, moves through loop 3, turns east to pass once more through station 2—this time on a different track. It continues on to the overpass 4 and from there into loops 5 and 6. From there it returns to overpass 4 and from there it retraces its earlier route until it gets back to station 1—this time facing north. After an (optional) stop, it continues north and then south through loop 9. Then it travels west all the way to loops 7 and 8. From there it turns east and south to loop 3, on the outer track, continues through overpass 4 and loops 5 and 6, goes back to stations 2, and again faces north when arriving at station 1.

Assuming that the train travels at an average scale speed of 35 mph, the operation I have described should take roughly 20 minutes. With that much track at your disposal, it would be fairly easy to operate a second and possibly even a third train simultaneously without causing interference. And it would not necessarily require more than one operator to handle the whole thing.

This track plan offers virtually limitless possibilities for landscaping. Portions of the track can be hidden from view. This adds to your fascination as trains appear unexpectedly at one location or the other.

Type: Continuous Run		
Gauge	Layout in Feet	Track in Feet
O	120 x 67	1,380
S	90 x 50	1,035
OO	76 x 42	869
HO	66 x 37	761
TT	48 x 27	552
N	36 x 20	414

Turnouts
  Left Hand: 2
  Right Hand: 3
Crossings: 0 (14)
Stations: 2
Return Loops: 1

Scale Miles: 11.38
Running Time at 35 mph: 0:19:31

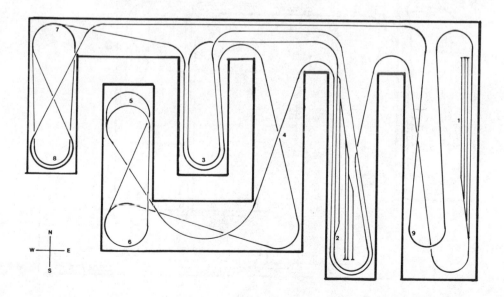

LAYOUT 46

Here is a layout that is designed around such unavoidable obstacles as furnaces, water heaters, or whatever else might be found in the average basement. While it has been designed for a fairly large area, it could easily be squeezed into half the space indicated without causing the curve radii to become prohibitively tight. This would necessarily reduce the total running time by something like 50 percent and reduce the amount of track needed by the same percentage.

Let's follow one train through and see where it goes. Assuming the train has been stored on tracks 1, facing east, it will move out through the inner track in loop 2 and then turn north and west on the third track from the top. When turning south, it will continue on the outer track in loop 5 and eventually head east again on the track that is closest to the north edge of the layout. Once arriving opposite loop 4, the train can either continue on south and back to loop 2 for a repeat of the same route or it can turn east. Turning east will also bring it back to the route just traveled.

When it returns to the southbound track, it ends up in station 6. It will now either have to back out or it can use the connecting track to loop 5, the inner track. From there, it can either continue to travel between loops 4 and 5 or it can use the single crossover that will take it back to loops 2 and 3, and eventually station 1.

By installing additional crossovers, the variety of operations can be increased. That will also require considerably more attention on the part of the operator. This is especially true if several trains are to be operated at the same time.

Type: Continuous Run		
Gauge	Layout in Feet	Track in Feet
O	113 x 73	1,437
S	85 x 55	1,078
OO	71 x 46	905
HO	62 x 40	792
TT	45 x 29	575
N	34 x 22	431

Turnouts
  Left Hand: 5
  Right Hand: 4
  Single Crossover: 1
Crossings: 0 (16)
Stations: 2
Return Loops: 2

Scale Miles: 11.85
Running Time at 35 mph: 0:20:19

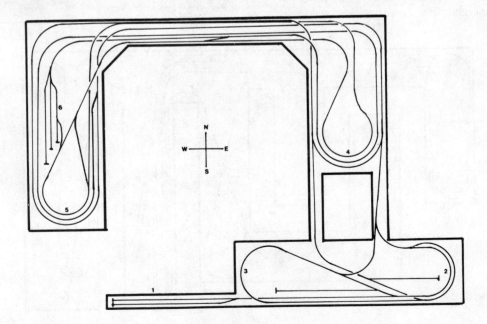

LAYOUT 47

Here is a large layout that can be used either for point-to-point operation between two stations or for continuous operation of several trains. This layout, too, could be squeezed into a smaller space. In the smaller gauges, it would fit into a garage or basement.

Assuming a train leaves westward from station 1, it will go south through loop 2 and continue on north and east to loop 5. Here it will either return to station 1 or continue on south past station 7, turning north and then west and south, eventually reaching loop 3. Here it can either continue on straight, returning to station 7, or it can make use of the crossover that would lead it into the return loop 6. Then it would retrace the steps described earlier but in the opposite direction.

Clever landscaping could be used to hide some of the long, parallel main lines from view. This makes the operation more fascinating to the average observer.

Type: Continuous Run		
Gauge	Layout in Feet	Track in Feet
O	106 x 73	2,680
S	80 x 55	2,010
OO	67 x 46	1,688
HO	59 x 40	1,477
TT	43 x 29	1,072
N	32 x 22	804

Turnouts
 Left Hand: 2
 Right Hand: 2
 Single Crossover: 2
Crossings: 0 (11)
Stations: 2
Return Loops: 1

Scale Miles: 22.1
Running Time at 35 mph: 0:37:53

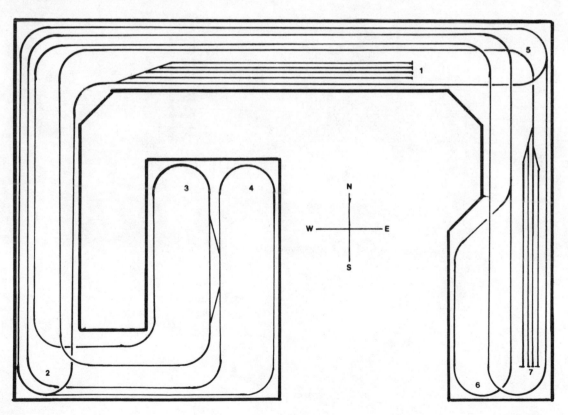

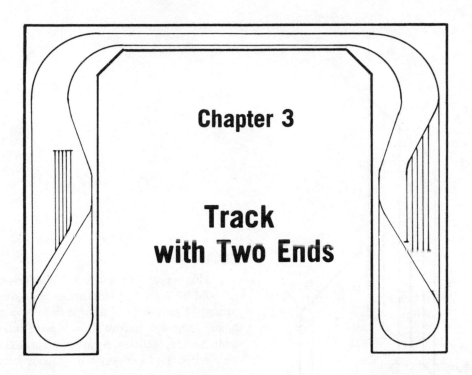

Chapter 3

Track
with Two Ends

In the real world, trains don't run around in circles or ovals. Because model railroaders simply don't have the space to realistically reproduce the tracks over long distances, it is often difficult to construct point-to-point layouts that are even vaguely realistic. Compromise is the name of the game. The following pages provide track plans that are indicative of the kind of compromises that must be made if point-to-point operations are your primary interest.

Point-to-point operations are not for the armchair modeler. They require a lot of attention on the part of the operator. Trains arrive and leave. Whether they are on a specific schedule is beside the point. On the more complicated layouts, it is often necessary or, at least advisable, to have individual operators control individual trains.

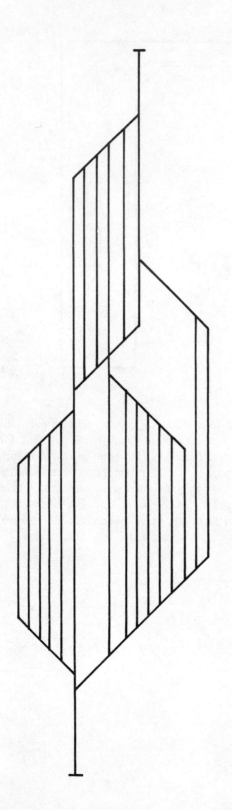

LAYOUT 48

This is really not a layout at all. Nevertheless, it could be stretched lengthwise and possibly repeated at two ends of a main line for a point-to-point, long and narrow layout with many yard-switching capabilities. A yard, similar to this, could be incorporated into any one of many layouts.

Type:	Point-to-Point	
Stations		1
Remarks:		

    Primarily, this is a schematic representation of a freight yard. It is intended to be used in conjunction with other layouts.

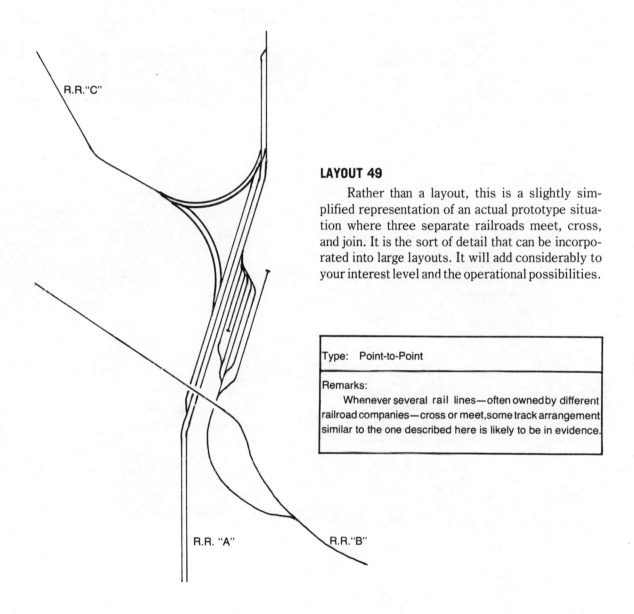

R.R."C"

R.R. "A"

R.R."B"

LAYOUT 49

Rather than a layout, this is a slightly simplified representation of an actual prototype situation where three separate railroads meet, cross, and join. It is the sort of detail that can be incorporated into large layouts. It will add considerably to your interest level and the operational possibilities.

Type: Point-to-Point
Remarks: Whenever several rail lines—often owned by different railroad companies—cross or meet, some track arrangement similar to the one described here is likely to be in evidence.

LAYOUT 50

Very often modelers find they are left with corners on a layout that remain unused. Here is a suggestion of how to use such a corner. Turn it into an engine storage facility surrounded by a return loop. Depending on the minimum radius you are willing to accept, this sort of thing can be squeezed into a relatively small space.

Type:	Point-to-Point
Remarks:	It is often possible to place a return loop around a turntable in the corner of a layout.

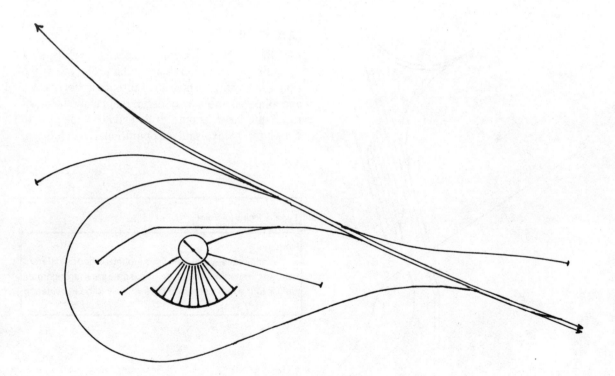

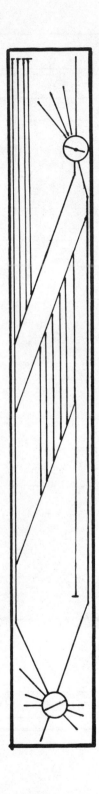

LAYOUT 51

This is about as simple a point-to-point layout as can be squeezed into a very narrow space. Nearly anyone who is interested in model railroading, but is cramped for space, can find a foot or so along the wall of one room where a shelf for such a layout could be installed.

Except for those modelers who prefer switching back and forth (coupling and uncoupling cars), to continuous running, this layout doesn't offer many operational possibilities. But under certain circumstances it may be better than nothing. An ambitious modeler might consider automating both turntables. While not adding a great deal to the operations, this will most probably keep a modeler out of mischief for a considerable period of time.

Type: Point-to-Point		
Gauge	Layout in Feet	Track in Feet
O	90 x 8	180
S	68 x 6	135
OO	57 x 5	113
HO	50 x 4.5	99
TT	36 x 3	72
N	27 x 2.5	54

Turnouts
  Left Hand:
  Right Hand:
  Three Way:
  Single Crossover: optional
  Double Crossover:
  Slip Switch:
Stations: 2

Scale Miles: 1.48
Running Time at 35 mph: 0:02:33

LAYOUT 52

Here is a point-to-point layout that fits into a reasonably small space. It accommodates three separate stations. Preferably, the stations should be separated visually by appropriate landscaping or structures. Operations, while limited by the available space, could be made interesting by having several operators control more than one train at a time as each moves according to some sort of schedule from one station to another.

Type: Point-to-Point		
Gauge	Layout in Feet	Track in Feet
O	25 x 15	97
S	19 x 11	73
OO	16 x 9	61
HO	14 x 8	53
TT	10 x 6	39
N	7.5 x 4.5	29

Turnouts
  Left Hand: 5
  Right Hand: 4
  Single Crossover: 1
Stations: 3

Scale Miles: 0.8
Running Time at 35 mph: 0:01:22

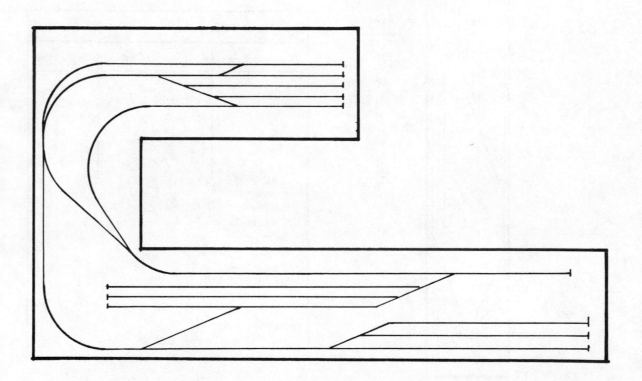

LAYOUT 53

This layout goes around three and three-fourths walls of a room if there is not sufficient space to widen it to include a complete turnaround. The one concession made is the space used by the wye; this makes it possible to reverse direction of the engines. Actually, there are two wyes. The other one is a kind of malformed affair located in the southeast corner.

With four stations and the profusion of spurs leading to mines or other industrial locations, this layout presents considerable operational opportunities for the modeler who likes to run trains from point X to point Y and so on.

If a removable section across the door in the northwest corner is added, the layout can be converted into one permitting continuous run around the periphery of the room.

Type: Point-to-Point		
Gauge	Layout in Feet	Track in Feet
O	57 x 37	140
S	43 x 28	105
OO	36 x 23	88
HO	31 x 20	77
TT	23 x 15	56
N	17 x 11	42

Turnouts
  Left Hand:
  Right Hand:
  Three Way: optional
  Single Crossover:
  Double Crossover:
  Slip Switch:
Stations: 3
Wyes: 2

Scale Miles: 1.15
Running Time at 35 mph: 0:01:59

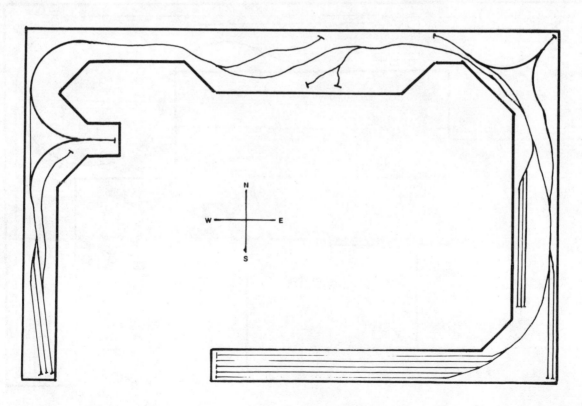

LAYOUT 54

This point-to-point layout accommodates four stations located on several levels. In order to accomplish the level changes without resorting to excessively steep grades, you will probably have to make the northeast portion of the circle in the northeast corner of the layout somewhat higher than the southwest corner of that circle. In addition, you can elevate the tracks in station 1, especially the one leading to point A even a bit more.

Stations 2 and 3 are likely to end up on different levels, which is just as well, as this will simplify the task of masking one from the other by such means as landscaping, structures, or backdrop.

I am assuming that you will make the section with the turntable, shown in the insert, *above* the portion containing circle 6. It could also be built below, but turntable action is not only interesting to watch, it is also an operation in which you will need to observe.

Type: Point-to-Point		
Gauge	Layout in Feet	Track in Feet
O	57 x 40	193
S	43 x 30	145
OO	36 x 25	122
HO	31 x 22	107
TT	23 x 16	77
N	17 x 12	58

Turnouts
  Left Hand: 3
  Right Hand: 2
Stations: 2
Wyes: 1

Scale Miles: 1.59
Running Time at 35 mph: 0:02:44

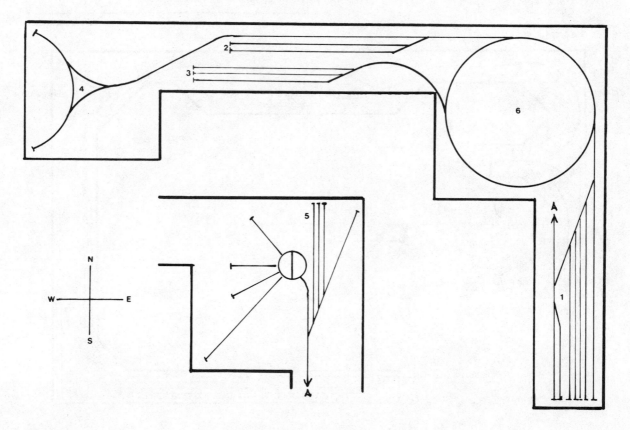

LAYOUT 55

This layout is more or less a starter layout. It will provide the beginner with experience in building, landscaping, and limited operation, but after a while it will likely become simply a portion of an expanded track plan.

In its initial design, it was simply a length of track with a station at each end. The track doubles back over itself in the northeast oval in order to increase the running time between stations. To make it a bit more interesting, you could add a passing siding (the dashed line) to make it possible to run two trains in opposite directions at the same time.

An additional option is the inclusion of a wye in order to be able to turn engines around without having to pick them up. The dotted line at point 3 shows how such a wye could be incorporated without having to add any layout space.

This is the sort of track plan that is ideally suited to teach track-laying technique, to demonstrate how the percentages of grades must be carefully figured in order to be sure that one track is high enough at a given point to pass safely over the other, and there is ample opportunity to try your hand at some interesting landscaping.

Type: Point-to-Point		
Gauge	Layout in Feet	Track in Feet
O	47 x 33	290
S	35 x 25	218
OO	29 x 21	183
HO	26 x 18	160
TT	19 x 13	116
N	14 x 10	87

Turnouts
  Left Hand: 1, 3, or 4
  Right Hand: 1, 2, or 3
Crossings: 0 (2)
Stations: 2
Wyes: 1 (optional)

Scale Miles: 2.39
Running Time at 35 mph: 0:04:06

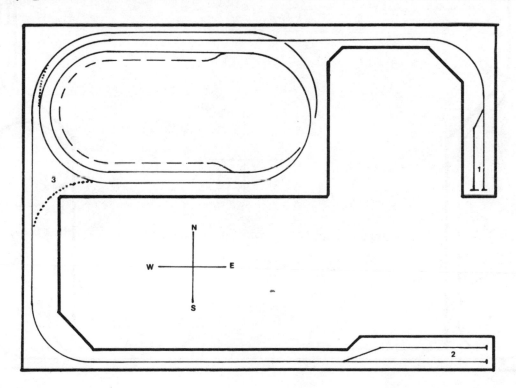

LAYOUT 56

Here is an around-the-wall layout consisting of two stations and a single main line. Two return loops have been added to make it possible at each end to turn the train around and have it re-enter the main line in the opposite direction. If there is sufficient room at the narrow east side of the layout, a passing siding could be added to permit running two trains at the same time.

As the layout is shown, continuous operation would not be possible. A train could start at the south station, go around the loop at the north station, and return to the south station. But then it would have to back through the return loop in the south in order to again be able to go north. That problem could be rectified by changing the design of the loop at the south station to be identical to the one in the north. If that is done, continuous operation will be possible assuming the operator is on his toes each time the train re-enters the main line in the opposite direction. A reversal of the electric current at the right moment is required.

Type: Point-to-Point		
Gauge	Layout in Feet	Track in Feet
O	50 x 30	157
S	38 x 23	118
OO	31 x 19	99
HO	28 x 17	86
TT	20 x 12	63
N	15 x 9	47

Turnouts
  Left Hand: 6
  Right Hand: 4
Stations: 2
Return Loops: 2

Scale Miles: 1.29
Running Time at 35 mph: 0:02:13

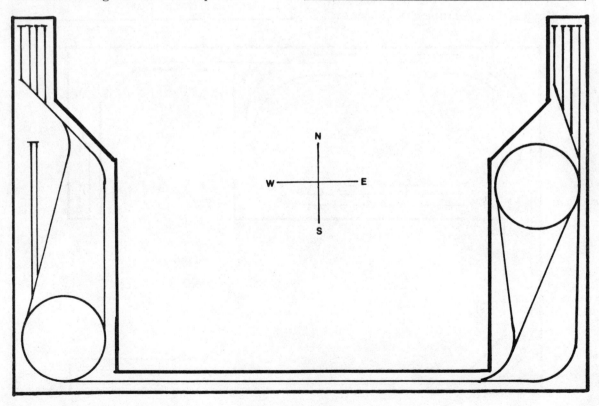

LAYOUT 57

Here is a series of five schematic illustrations showing how a simple point-to-point track plan can be converted progressively to one that incorporates all of the same features, but that also permits continuous operation. In the final versions, reverse direction of travel is possible.

Figure 3-1 shows a schematic representation of a typical prototype situation. A track runs from one station to another with a siding, several spurs, and some yard tracks along the way. While a layout like that could be built, it is my feeling that operating it would soon prove to be rather boring.

Figure 3-2 shows the identical track plan bent into a horseshoe in order to be able to place it around the walls of a room. While this might make it more adaptable to the space that might be available to the average modeler, it in no way improves the operational possibilities.

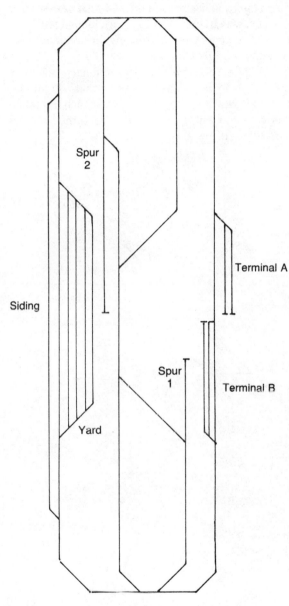

Type:	Point-to-Point	
	Out and Return	
	Continuous Run	

Gauge	Layout in Feet	Track in Feet
O	60 x 20	410
S	45 x 15	308
OO	38 x 13	258
HO	33 x 11	226
TT	24 x 8	164
N	18 x 6	123

Turnouts
  Left Hand:
  Right Hand:
  Three Way:
  Single Crossover: } progressive
  Double Crossover:
  Slip Switch:
Stations: 2
Return Loops: 0,1,2

Scale Miles: 3.38
Running Time at 35 mph: 0:05:48

Figure 3-3 shows the track bent back onto itself, connecting one of the tracks in the two stations.

While this is not exactly realistic, it would be an easy matter, using appropriate landscaping and structures, to mask the fact that the two stations are actually connected. The purpose, of course, is to permit continuous running of a train. The spurs and the yard tracks are still in place, but the passing siding has been moved for space reasons. At this stage, the layout permits continuous running in one direction or the other, but it does not provide an opportunity to reverse direction of travel.

Figure 3-4 is identical to the one described previously, but an additional length of track connects the two spurs to make it possible to reverse the direction of train travel at once. But that is it. Once the train has passed through that new section of track, which represents a return loop, it will have to continue operating in the new direction because it cannot be turned around again.

Figure 3-5 corrects the directional problem by adding some new track sections and, of course, turnouts. Now you have a layout on which trains can run continuously, and they can be turned around regardless of the direction of travel.

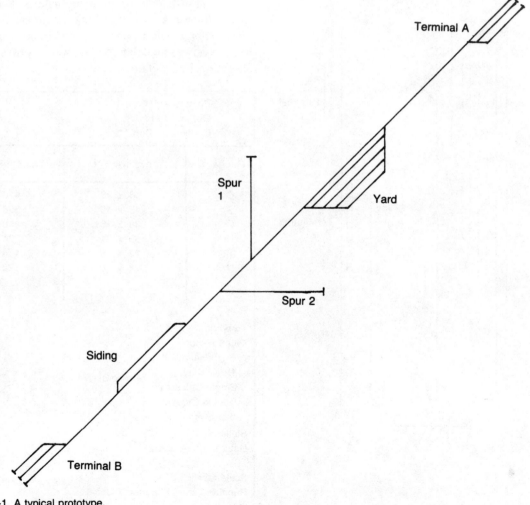

Fig. 3-1. A typical prototype.

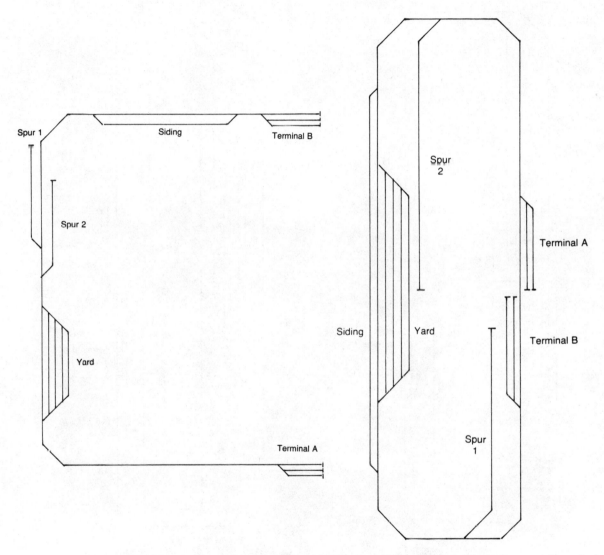

Fig. 3-2. A horseshoe layout.

Fig. 3-3. The track bent back onto itself.

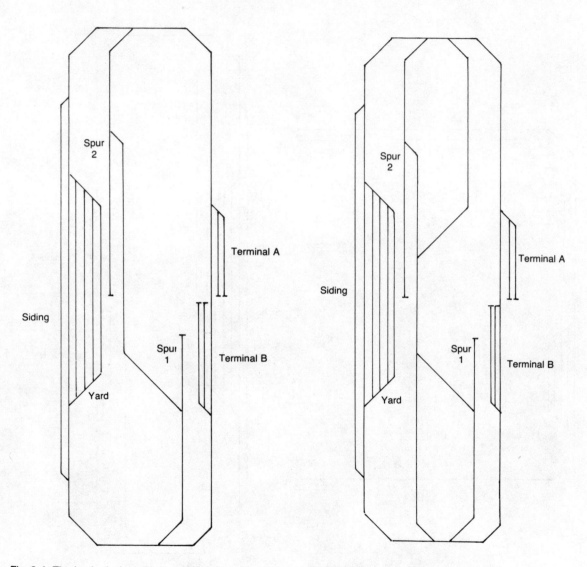

Fig. 3-4. The basic design with an additional length of track.   Fig. 3-5. New track and turnouts.

LAYOUT 58

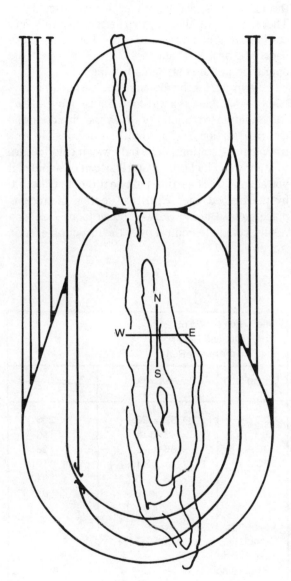

For all practical purposes, here is simply a combination of a figure eight and an oval. By combining those two features, you have a layout that can be used for point-to-point operation. It can also permit continuous running and the reversal of train travel in either direction.

A train can move south from the west station, come around the outer south loop, and then head north and left into the north loop. It can then run around the oval indefinitely or it can go through the two middle turnouts and reverse direction. Alternately, it can go to either the east or the west station and stop there.

The purpose of the lightly indicated mountain range in the center, running from north to south, is to screen the two stations from one another and to mask the unrealistic symmetry of the layout as a whole. Despite its relatively small size, this layout accommodates quite a few operational possibilities without requiring excessively tight curves.

Type:	Point-to-Point Continuous Run	
Gauge	Layout in Feet	Track in Feet
O	27 x 13	240
S	20 x 10	180
OO	17 x 8	151
HO	15 x 7	132
TT	11 x 5	96
N	8 x 4	72

Turnouts
Left Hand: 3
Right Hand: 2
Y: 2
Crossings: 0 (1)
Stations: 2
Return Loops: 2
Wyes: 1

Scale Miles: 1.98
Running Time at 35 mph: 0:03:24

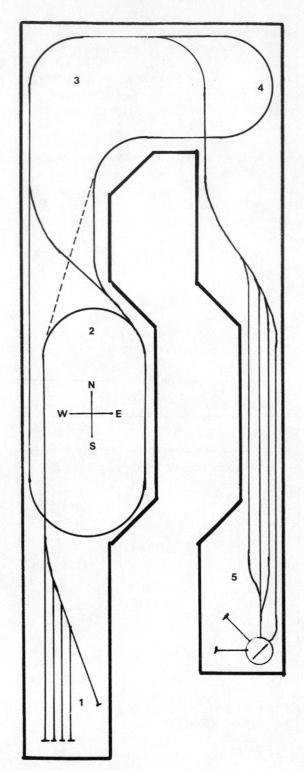

LAYOUT 59

This track plan combines point-to-point, out-and return, and continuous-run operations. As originally drawn, a train would leave station 1, go through oval 2, and continue on toward curve 3. There it could either turn right and go south into station 5 or it could go on to curve 4 and from there back into oval 2. From there it would repeat the operation in the continuous-run mode.

Ignoring, for the moment, the dashed line, it is obvious that there is a way for a train leaving station 5 to either go to station 1 or to reverse direction and return to station 5. That would not be possible for a train leaving station 1. The only way it could return to station 1 is by backing up. This can be avoided if you add the track section and two turnouts indicated by the dashed line. With that section of track in place, you would have two return loops and, as a result, complete control over the direction of train travel.

Type:	Point-to-Point	
	Out and Return	
	Continuous Run	

Gauge	Layout in Feet	Track in Feet
O	57 x 20	203
S	43 x 15	153
OO	36 x 13	128
HO	31 x 11	112
TT	23 x 8	81
N	17 x 6	61

Turnouts	
Left Hand:	1
Right Hand:	2
Crossings:	2
Stations:	2
Return Loops:	1

Scale Miles: 1.68
Running Time at 35 mph: 0:02:52

LAYOUT 60

The two track plans shown in this layout are actually one layout designed to be placed on two levels, one above the other. This is basically a point-to-point operation with the possibility of lengthening the time between stations by using a hidden section that permits continuous running as well as reversal of the direction of travel.

The figure eight plus oval portion of the layout should be hidden beneath the one with the stations. The double line represents a background board or some other type of screening through landscaping or structures to hide the two stations from each other.

A train can leave the station on the far left, go around the oval track, and then disappear at point B. It will enter the lower portion at point B and spend time out of sight. It can then either exit at point A to eventually reach the other station or it can reverse direction and exit through point B and return to the station from which it started.

If the two sections were offset by, for example, a third of the width of the layout, some of the lower operation would be visible and available for landscaping.

Type:	Point-to-Point	
	Continuous Run	
Gauge	Layout in Feet	Track in Feet
O	33 x 17	227
S	25 x 12.5	170
OO	21 x 10.5	143
HO	18 x 9	125
TT	13 x 6.5	91
N	10 x 5	68

Turnouts
  Left Hand: 4
  Right Hand: 4
Crossings: 1 (+1)
Stations: 2
Return Loops: 2

Two-Level Layout
Scale Miles: 1.87
Running Time at 35 mph: 0:03:12

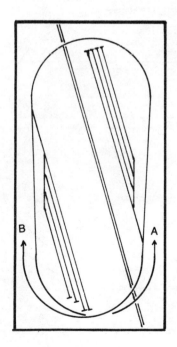

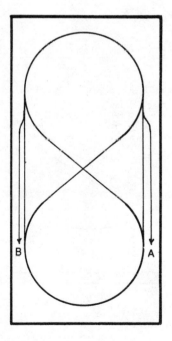

LAYOUT 61

When very little space is available, there isn't an awful lot that can be done without getting involved with curves that are too sharp to accommodate some of the larger types of rolling stock that many of us like. Here we have a very small layout that includes three stations and one return loop, plus the capability to run a train continuously.

A train leaving station 2 can use the return loop in order to get back to where it came from or it can move into the other track and either run continuously or pull into station 3. A train leaving station 3 can only go on to station 2 or run continuously. It cannot be turned around.

| Type: | Point-to-Point | |
| | Continuous Run | |

Gauge	Layout in Feet	Track in Feet
O	19 x 11	70
S	14 x 8	53
OO	12 x 7	44
HO	10 x 6	39
TT	7 x 4	28
N	5.5 x 3.5	21

Turnouts
  Left Hand: 1
  Right Hand: 4
  Y: 1
Crossings: 3
Stations: 2
Return Loops: 1

Scale Miles: 0.58
Running Time at 35 mph: 0:00:59

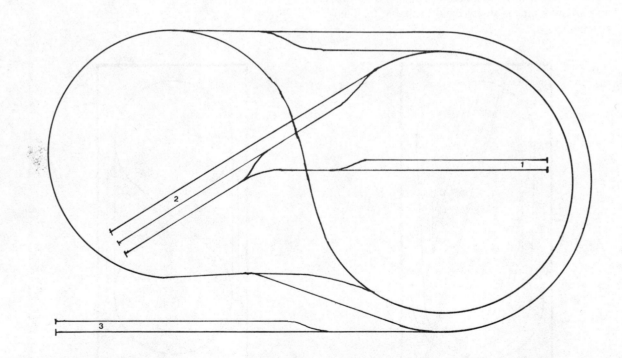

LAYOUT 62

This layout is designed for an L-shaped space of limited proportions. It consists of two stations, two passing sidings, and a turned-upon-itself oval to permit continuous running of trains in addition to point-to-point operation. There are no return loops and the only means of reversing the direction of a train would be to uncouple the engine, take it to the turntable, turn it around, and then couple it to the other end of the train.

If the overpass between points 4 and 2 would be made into a crossing, it would be possible to place a turnout at the point identified as 4. The other track from that turnout would then run north and join the north-south track at the far west side of the layout. This would permit reversing the direction of trains in one direction but not in the other. In other words, a train leaving station 2, northbound, could then move directly into curve 4. This will permit it to return to station 2 in the opposite direction.

Type:	Point-to-Point Continuous Run	
Gauge	Layout in Feet	Track in Feet
O	27 x 17	137
S	20 x 13	103
OO	17 x 10	86
HO	15 x 9	75
TT	11 x 7	55
N	8 x 5	41

Turnouts
  Left Hand: 3
  Right Hand: 3
Crossings: 0 (1)
Stations: 2

Scale Miles: 1.13
Running Time at 35 mph: 0:01:56

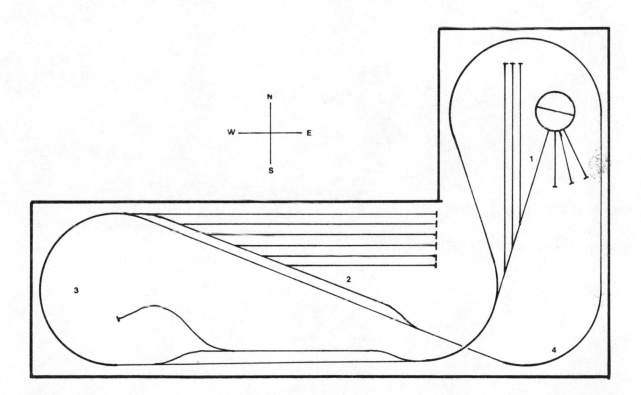

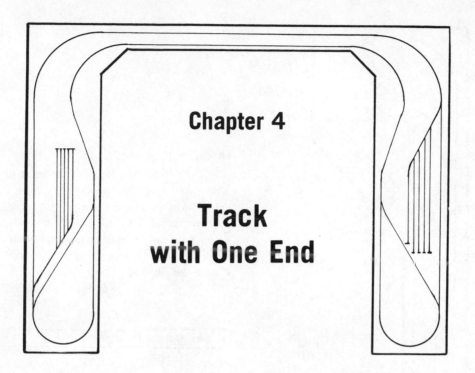

Chapter 4

Track
with One End

This chapter contains layouts designed for out-and-return operations. This is really just a variation on the point-to-point operations except that here point 1 and point 2 are the same. To put it another way, a train leaves the station, covers a certain length of main line, and then returns to where it came from.

On its return trip, the train will be facing head first into a dead end. Therefore, it is often a good idea to include a wye or, space permitting, a return loop to permit the operator to turn the train around without having to physically pick it up and then put it back on the tracks facing in the opposite direction. The only alternative would be to have the train make the next trip traveling backward. That way it will arrive at the station facing out.

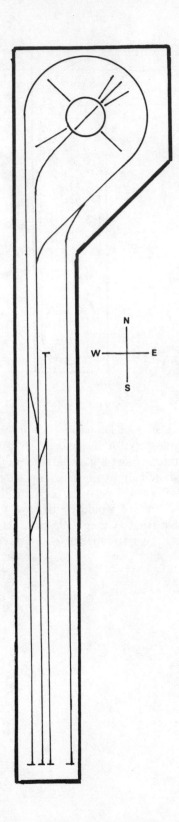

LAYOUT 63

This is a very simple out-and-return layout with a station on one end and the space in the return curve used to accommodate a turntable. If a modeler wanted to, he could use landscaping or structures to visually separate the track on the west side of the layout from that on the east side. This would create the illusion of two stations.

Type: Out and Return		
Gauge	Layout in Feet	Track in Feet
O	63 x 7	140
S	48 x 5	105
OO	40 x 4	88
HO	35 x 4	77
TT	25 x 3	56
N	19 x 2	42

Turnouts
  Left Hand: 1
  Right Hand: 1
  Single Crossover: 3
Stations: 1
Return Loops: 1

Scale Miles: 1.15
Running Time at 35 mph: 0:01:59

LAYOUT 64

Here is an out-and-return layout with a number of added attractions. Basically, there is a station and a convoluted section of main line. The main line is designed to permit continuous running of a train. In addition, at point 3, there is a wye that permits you to turn the train around. But there is more. Assuming the modeler would prefer to have two stations, he or she could erect a visual barrier between tracks 1 and 2. Pronto! You would have two stations instead of one.

Type:	Out and Return	
Gauge	Layout in Feet	Track in Feet
O	53 x 27	177
S	40 x 20	133
OO	34 x 17	111
HO	29 x 15	97
TT	21 x 11	71
N	16 x 8	53

Turnouts
  Left Hand: 1
  Y: 3
  Single Crossover: 2
Crossings: 0 (3)
Stations: 1
Return Loops: 1
Wyes: 1
Scale Miles: 1.46
Running Time at 35 mph: 0:02:30

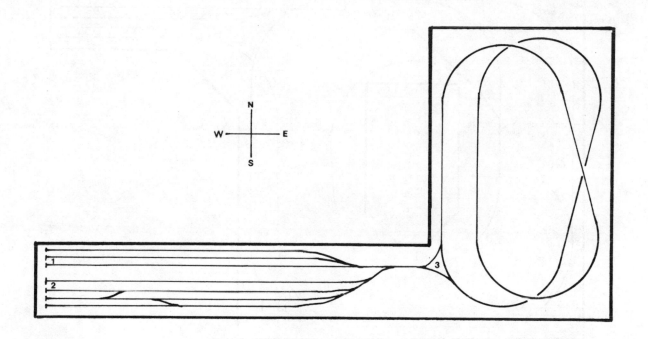

LAYOUT 65

This plan is not too different from the previous layout. It involves a station for out-and-return operation and a main line that permits continuous running of one train.

The tracks that represent the station can be separated into two groups—divided by some type of visual barrier—to give the impression that there are actually two stations rather than one. As shown, there is no wye or other means of reversing the direction of train travel. Depending on the space available, either a wye or a turntable could be added.

Type:	Out and Return	
	Continuous Run	
Gauge	Layout in Feet	Track in Feet
O	28 x 18	130
S	21 x 14	98
OO	18 x 12	82
HO	16 x 10	72
TT	11 x 7	52
N	8.5 x 5.5	39

Turnouts
  Left Hand: 2
  Right Hand: 3
Crossings: 2
Stations: 1
Return Loops: 1

Scale Miles: 1.07
Running Time at 35 mph: 0:01:50

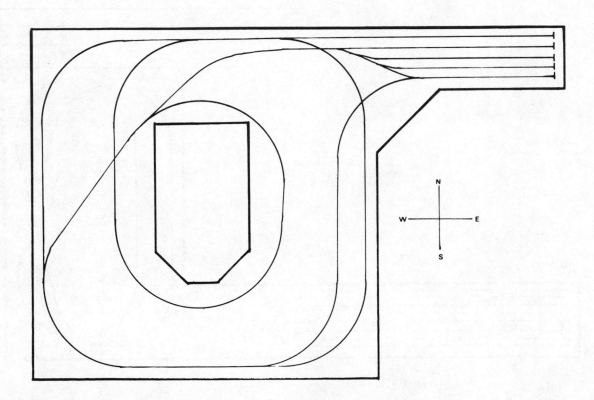

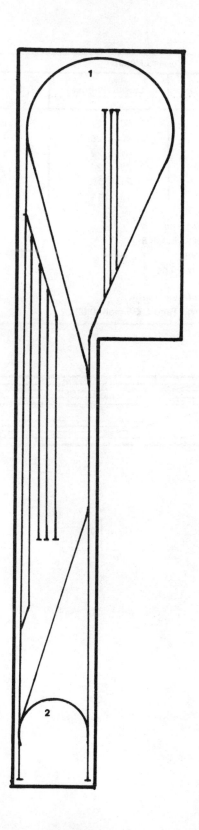

LAYOUT 66

Here is a skinny layout that incorporates two stations, a return loop (1), and a wye (2). For modelers who delight in complicated switching operations, there are ample challenges considering the amount of space involved.

Type:	Out and Return	
Gauge	Layout in Feet	Track in Feet
O	60 x 13	150
S	45 x 10	113
OO	38 x 8	94
HO	33 x 7	83
TT	24 x 5	60
N	18 x 4	45

Turnouts
  Left Hand: 4
  Right Hand: 1
  Three Way: 1
Stations: 2
Return Loops: 1
Wyes: 1

Scale Miles: 1.24
Running Time at 35 mph: 0:02:07

LAYOUT 67

As originally drawn, this is strictly an out-and-return situation. The train leaves the station, moves into the main line, and returns to the station. With the tracks in the station itself, and the industrial or mining spurs, there are a number of operational possibilities. Nevertheless, they remain limited. See Fig. 4-1.

By adding the sections of track represented by the two dashed lines, the train could operate continuously within the limits of the oval that is created by those dashed lines.

Type:	Out and Return	
Gauge	Layout in Feet	Track in Feet
O	53 x 37	173
S	40 x 28	130
OO	34 x 23	109
HO	29 x 20	96
TT	21 x 15	69
N	16 x 11	52

Turnouts
  Left Hand: 5
  Right Hand: 3
Stations: 1
Return Loops: 1

Scale Miles: 1.43
Running Time at 35 mph: 0:02:27

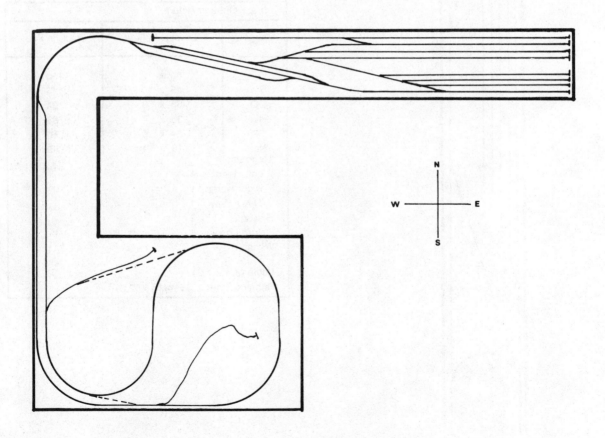

Fig. 4-1. By having many tracks run parallel interest can be added to an out-anc-return layout.

LAYOUT 68

This track plan is designed to keep the operator on his or her toes. Basically, there is one station and three return loops. The train can leave the station on the south side of the layout, go straight north past the passing siding, through loop 1, and curve 4, and into loop 3. It can then either retrace its steps or it can move into loop 2, and then return either to the station or go again through loop 3.

Loops 2 and 3 or loops 2 and 1, including curve 4, each represent an opportunity for continuous running of a train. This does involve repeated changing of turnout alignments and reversals of the direction of the electrical current.

With the appropriate landscaping, this layout could easily provide hours of exciting fun.

Type:	Out and Return	
Gauge	Layout in Feet	Track in Feet
O	47 x 37	290
S	35 x 28	218
OO	29 x 23	183
HO	26 x 20	160
TT	19 x 15	116
N	14 x 11	87

Turnouts:
  Left Hand: 4
  Right Hand: 5
Stations: 1
Return Loops: 1

Scale Miles: 2.39
Running Time at 35 mph: 0:04:06

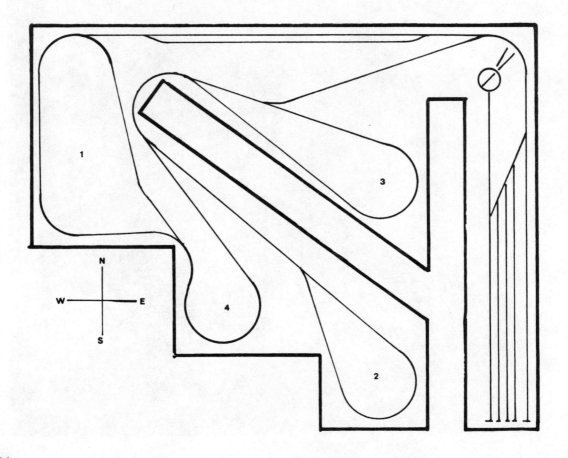

LAYOUT 69

This medium-sized layout permits out-and-return and point-to-point operations. No provision is made for the continuous running of trains. Incorporated are two or possibly three stations and two return loops. In the event that you prefer to have three (rather than two) stations, the tracks identified as 1 and 2 must be separated by some type of visual barrier.

A train leaving station 1, going east and then north, can be directed to the northbound track at the far east side of the layout. In such a case, it will enter the return loop 4 and eventually retrace its steps. It will either return to station 1 or be switched to station 2. In the event that the turnout at the southeast corner of the layout was set to take the train to the northbound center track, it will move through area 5 and continue underneath station 3, eventually reaching station 2.

As the layout is shown, it will not be possible to go directly from station 1 to station 3. The latter station can only be reached from station 2. This could, of course, be remedied by placing a crossover between the two inner parallel northbound tracks.

Type:	Out and Return	
Gauge	Layout in Feet	Track in Feet
O	28 x 18	227
S	21 x 14	170
OO	18 x 12	143
HO	16 x 10	125
TT	11 x 7	91
N	8.5 x 5.5	68

Turnouts
  Left Hand: 5
  Right Hand: 2
Crossings: 0 (6)
Stations: 2
Return Loops: 1

Scale Miles: 1.87
Running Time at 35 mph: 0:03:12

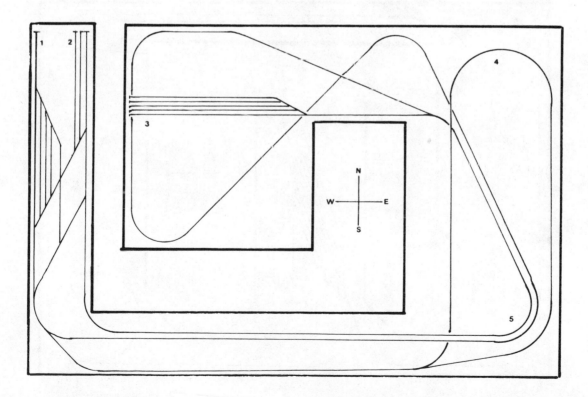

LAYOUT 70

This layout is designed exclusively for out and return operation. It would be possible to have two trains leave station 1; one would turn south and the other would turn north. They would pass each other in the passing siding on the west side of the layout before returning to station 1. Alternately, the train that initially turned south can reverse direction either in loop 2 or in loop 3 and return the way it came. This is not true of the train that turned north after leaving the station. It has no opportunity to reverse direction.

By making two relatively minor changes, involving four additional turnouts, it would be possible to increase the variety of available operations. One change would call for a connecting track at the point marked 4. Such a track would permit continuous running of the trains. A similar addition at the point marked 5 would make it possible for a train traveling northbound, out of station 1, to reverse direction in loop 2 and then retrace its steps.

Type:	Out and Return	
Gauge	Layout in Feet	Track in Feet
O	47 x 33	257
S	35 x 25	193
OO	29 x 21	162
HO	26 x 18	141
TT	19 x 13	103
N	14 x 10	77

Turnouts
  Left Hand: 3
  Right Hand: 6
  Y   1
Stations: 1
Return Loops: 2

Scale Miles: 2.12
Running Time at 35 mph: 0:03:38

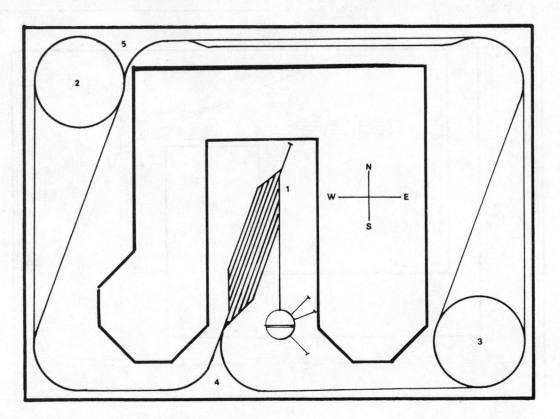

LAYOUT 71

This layout has a considerable variety of operational possibilities. In the smaller scales, it would fit into the average two-car garage. It incorporates three stations and a sufficient number of return loops to permit changing the direction of travel of several trains when more than one train is being run simultaneously.

Starting from station 1, a train could either go directly to station 3 or it could bypass that station and move through curve 7 into station 2. Or it could simply return to where it came from. Alternately, it could run continuously through curves 4, 5, 6, and 8 until the operator decides to switch it into any of the three stations.

This is a layout that seems to cry out for the simultaneous use of two or even three trains. The result can be truly exciting train movements.

Type:	Out and Return	
	Continuous Run	
Gauge	Layout in Feet	Track in Feet
O	127 x 67	737
S	95 x 50	553
OO	80 x 42	464
HO	70 x 37	406
TT	51 x 27	295
N	38 x 20	221

Turnouts
 Left Hand: 5
 Right Hand: 6
Crossings: 1
Stations: 3
Return Loops: 2

Scale Miles: 6.08
Running Time at 35 mph: 0:10:25

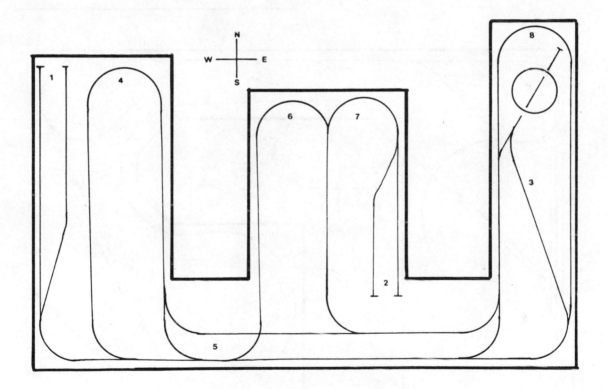

LAYOUT 72

Here is an out-and-return layout that also permits point-to-point operation. Continuous running cannot be accomplished without uninterrupted attention by the operator. It consists of two stations, a few optional spurs, and three return loops.

A train leaving station 1 can move through loop 4, reversing direction, and returning to station 1 or it could continue northbound, move through loop 3, and arrive at station 2. It could extend its main line run by traveling through loop 5. This will cause it to return to station 1.

Similarly, a train starting out of station 2 would have the same options of taking the long or short route to station 1 or of returning directly to station 2.

Type:	Out and Return	
Gauge	Layout in Feet	Track in Feet
O	53 x 33	303
S	40 x 25	228
OO	34 x 21	191
HO	29 x 18	167
TT	21 x 13	121
N	16 x 10	91

Turnouts
  Left Hand: 5
  Right Hand: 5
  Single Crossover: 3
Crossings: 0 (1)
Stations: 2
Return Loops: 2

Scale Miles: 2.5
Running Time at 35 mph: 0:04:17

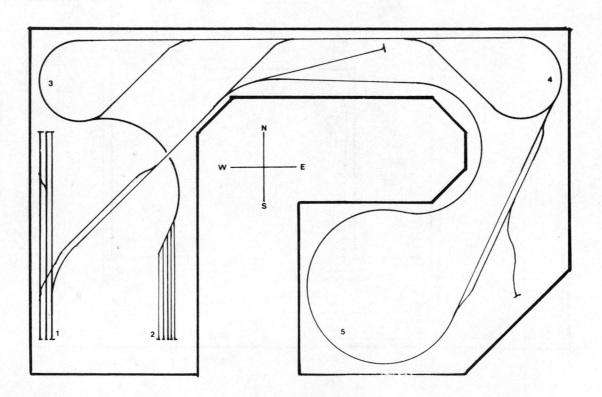

LAYOUT 73

This is the last and by far the most complicated of the out-and-return track plans. There are five separate stations, but only two of them can be reached directly without having to cover a length of convoluted main line. See Fig. 4-2.

The main line consists of all manner of loops upon loops. Someone adept at clever landscaping could hide portions of these loops to cause amazing visual results when trains appear and disappear at the most unexpected places. Just to get a feel for what is possible, let's follow several trains as they leave their respective stations.

A train leaving station 1 can go directly to station 5 while ignoring the rest of the main line altogether. Or it can turn south and enter curve 6, followed by curve 9, after which it will again end up in station 5. When leaving station 5, it could continue northbound and retrace its route through loop 9. When advancing on the double slip switch, it would be shunted into loop 8.

Continuing northbound, it would eventually

Type:	Out and Return	
Gauge	Layout in Feet	Track in Feet
O	50 x 37	610
S	38 x 28	458
OO	31 x 23	384
HO	28 x 20	336
TT	20 x 15	244
N	15 x 11	183

Turnouts
  Left Hand: 6
  Right Hand: 4
Slip Switch: 1
Crossings: 0 (25)
Stations: 5

Scale Miles: 5.03
Running Time at 35 mph: 0:08:37

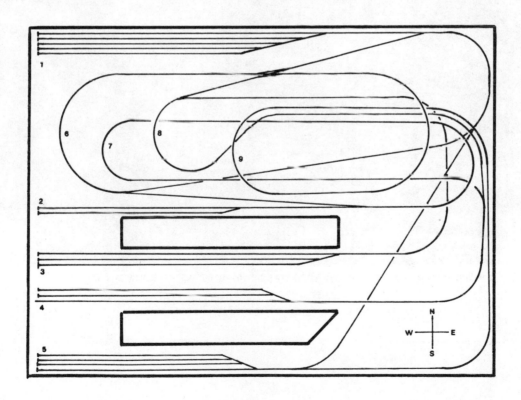

reach station 4. After taking on passengers or freight, it now leaves station 4, moves north, then west, and then directly south into loop 7. The train will eventually arrive at station 2.

So far there would be trains in stations 1, 2, 4, and 5. Station 3 would be left with no service. When the train left station 4, it could turn into loop 7, as was described above, or it could continue on, moving through loop 8 and then, (before reaching the double slip switch) turn right. This would have

caused it to arrive at station 3.

The challenge of this layout would be to start trains from two or three stations, at more or less the same time, and to give each a specific destination. Then each train will have to maneuver its way through the maze of convoluted loops and curves, occasionally waiting for another to pass or clear a track.

This layout is ideal for cab control with several operators each controlling just one train at a time.

Fig. 4-2. Interesting landscaping and structures along the right-of-way add appeal to any layout.

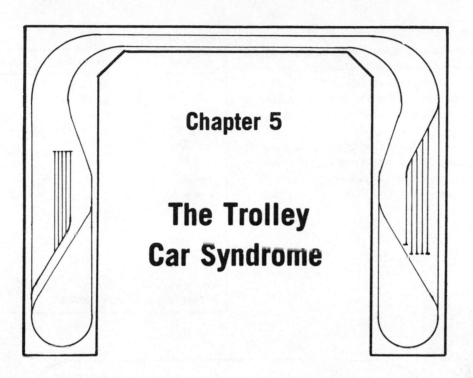

Chapter 5

The Trolley Car Syndrome

Many modelers, often those with limited space at their disposal, tend to lean toward creating an inner-city, trolley-car type of layout. Referred to as *traction* in model railroad parlance, these layouts can cram a great deal of operation into a small space. A trolley car can negotiate very sharp turns, and it rarely travels at speeds greater than 15 mph.

Other modelers like to combine traction portions on a layout with other sections on which regular trains perform the normal intercity operations. What follows is a small collection of such layout ideas. Some are limited to traction and others combine the two.

One thing should be kept in mind. To be realistic, traction operations require an overhead wire. Installing such overhead wires in a manner that permits the pantograph or trolley pole to actually make contact with that wire (even if it is not used to transmit electrical power) is not an easy task. This is especially true in the smaller gauges.

Another problem is that in some scales it is virtually impossible to obtain ready-to-run trolley cars from commercial manufacturers. The only alternatives are to build them from scratch or to try and modify some other type of engine such as a switcher with a short 0-4-0 wheelbase.

LAYOUT 74

This very small layout, which could easily fit on the average coffee table, has four city blocks and the streets on which the trolley cars will run. Despite its small size and the few feet of track used, it can give much pleasure in the variety of operations it offers.

As is true of all traction layouts, the modeler must be prepared to construct a sufficient number of buildings and structures to create the impression of a busy part of the city. See Figs. 5-1, 5-2 and 5-3.

Type: Traction		
Gauge	Layout in Feet	Track in Feet
0	10 x 10	87
S	8 x 8	65
OO	6 x 6	55
HO	5.5 x 5.5	48
TT	4 x 4	35
N	3 x 3	26

Turnouts:
  Left Hand: 1
  Right Hand: 2
  Y: 1
Crossings: 1
Return loops: 1

Scale Miles: 0.71
Running Time at 15 mph: 0:02:51

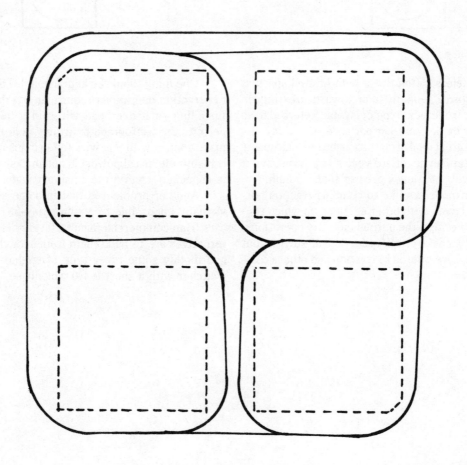

Fig. 5-1. This tiny traction layout was built to fit onto a coffee table.

Fig. 5-2. Structures, appropriate lighting, little figures, and automobiles add life to the street scene on this N-gauge traction layout.

Fig. 5-3. Sharp curves are acceptable on a traction layout, but overhead wires (not installed here) would add much to the realism of the scene.

LAYOUT 75

As is usually the case with traction layouts, the city with its streets, shopping centers, airports, city hall, and stadium had to be designed before any thought could be given to the actual track plan.

The rolling stock is stored in the car barn adjoining the interstate highway at the left. From there, the trolley cars can travel to the civic center, to the airport, and the shopping center. Additionally, in three places (two at the top and one at the bottom) provision has been made for future expansion of the layout.

Type: Traction		
Gauge	Layout in Feet	Track in Feet
O	47 x 40	207
S	35 x 30	155
OO	29 x 25	130
HO	26 x 22	113
TT	19 x 16	83
N	14 x 12	62

Turnouts:
  Left Hand: 5
  Right Hand: 4
Crossings: 1
Stations: 1

Scale Miles: 1.7
Running Time at 15 mph: 0:06:49

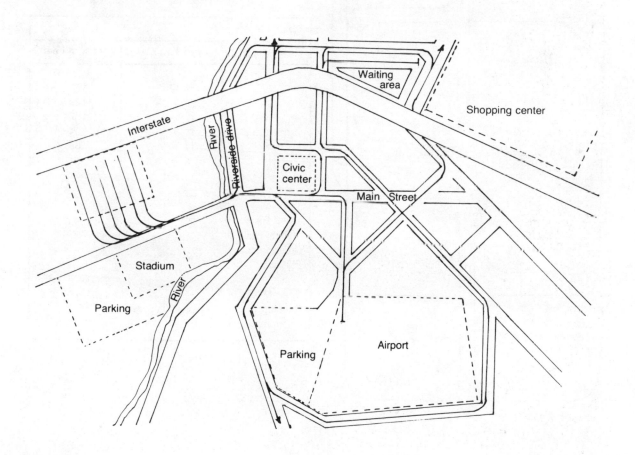

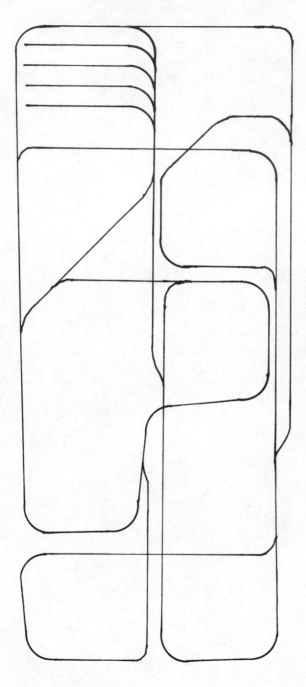

LAYOUT 76

This is another approach to a portion of a city. This one is designed to fit into a relatively long and narrow space. The first step was to model the city blocks and streets (Fig. 5-4). Then a track plan was designed to fit into that street layout. The intention is to permit continuously running operations over different sections of the track. Included is a car barn to store the rolling stock.

Type: Traction		
Gauge	Layout in Feet	Track in Feet
O	27 x 12	170
S	20 x 9	128
OO	17 x 7	107
HO	15 x 6	94
TT	11 x 5	68
N	8 x 3.5	51

Turnouts
　Left Hand: 5
　Right Hand: 8
Crossings: 6
Stations: 1

Scale Miles: 1.4
Running Time at 15 mph: 0:05:36

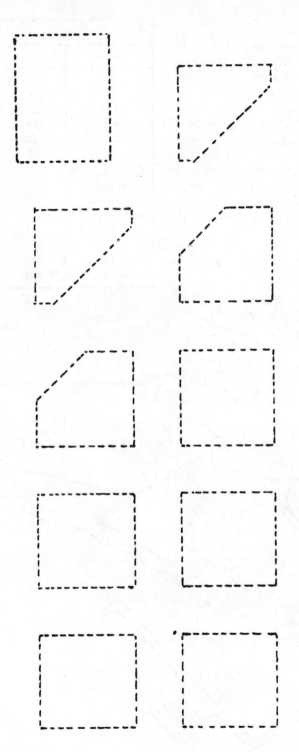

Fig. 5-4. The city blocks and streets.

LAYOUT 77

This layout was designed to be part of a larger railroad layout. It represents the trolley tracks that are limited to one of the towns on the larger layout.

These tracks lead from the car barn to the railroad station, around the city hall, across the railroad track, across the river to the public beach area, to the suburban shopping areas, and to the ball park. On its return trip, it also serves the industrial area by the railroad right-of-way. If you want to run the cars continuously, consider adding a bridge across the river at the right and connect the track leading to the ball park with the spur serving the railroad station.

Type:	Traction	
Gauge	Layout in Feet	Track in Feet
O	33 x 25	130
S	25 x 19	98
OO	21 x 16	82
HO	18 x 14	72
TT	13 x 10	52
N	10 x 7.5	39

Turnouts
  Left Hand: 4
  Right Hand: 4
Stations: 1
Return Loops: 1

Scale Miles: 1.07
Running Time at 15 mph: 0:04:17

LAYOUT 78

This somewhat more ambitious layout combines railroad operations with that of the streetcars. Figure 5-5 shows a relatively simple railroad layout surrounding a city area. The railroad station is at the bottom right and a small freight yard is directly above that area. The rest of the track is simply an oval that permits continuous running of the train. Also included is a return loop around the yard.

Figure 5-6 shows the street layout of the section of the city represented by the layout, West Street is on the left and First Street, Second Street, and Third Street are on the right leading out to other parts of the city and the suburbs.

Figure 5-7 is the track plan for the streetcar operation. It goes from the car barn to the railroad station. Along the way it serves most, though not all, parts of the city.

The three separate entities will fit together to provide ample opportunity for interesting operations and an exciting landscaping.

Type:	Continuous Run	
Gauge	Layout in Feet	
O	30 x 17	
S	23 x 13	
OO	19 x 10	
HO	17 x 9	
TT	12 x 7	
N	9 x 5	

Track in Feet		
Traction: 147	Railroad	87
110		65
92		55
81		48
57		35
44		26

Turnouts:	Left Hand:	Traction:	3	Railroad:	3
	Right Hand:		6		2
	Y:		3		0
	Slip Switch		1		0

Crossings:	1	Railroad:	0
Stations:	1		1
Return Loops:	1		1
Wyes:	1		0

Traction: Scale Miles: 1.21
      Running Time at 15 mph: 0:04:50

Railroad: Scale Miles: 0.71
      Running Time at 35 mph: 0:01:14

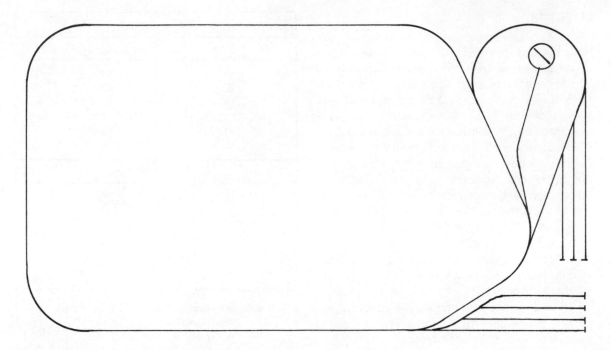

Fig. 5-5. The layout surrounding the city area.

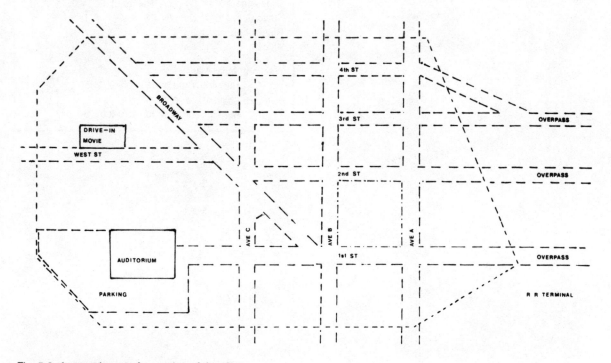

Fig. 5-6. A street layout of a section of the city.

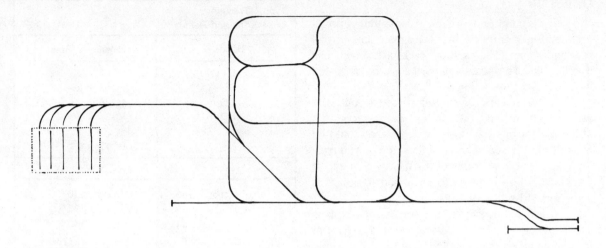

Fig. 5-7. The track plan for the streetcar operations.

LAYOUT 79

This is another approach to combining railroad and traction operations. In this example the railroad is predominant. The railroad tracks are shown as a double line. The streetcar tracks are represented by the single line.

At the southwest corner of the layout, the railroad station and the trolley tracks serve that station. East of it, at position 3, is what could be considered the old section of downtown. The trolley tracks serve portions of it. At the north end at position 2, there is a suburban railroad station. It is also served by the streetcar.

Both the railroad and the traction track plans are designed for out-and-return operations. Except for that small rectangle in downtown, neither would be able to keep on running continuously.

| Type: | Traction | |
| | Out and Return | |

Gauge	Layout in Feet
O	57 x 37
S	43 x 28
OO	36 x 23
HO	31 x 20
TT	23 x 15
N	17 x 11

Track in Feet			
Traction:	150	Railroad:	230
	113		173
	94		145
	83		127
	60		92
	45		69

Turnouts: Left Hand: Traction: 2   Railroad: 4
                 Right Hand: 2   4
                 Y: 2

Crossings: 1 (+3)
Stations: 2 and 2
Return Loops: 1 (Railroad)

Traction: Scale Miles: 1.24
          Running Time at 15 mph: 0:05:00
Railroad: Scale Miles: 1.89
          Running Time at 35 mph: 0:03:15

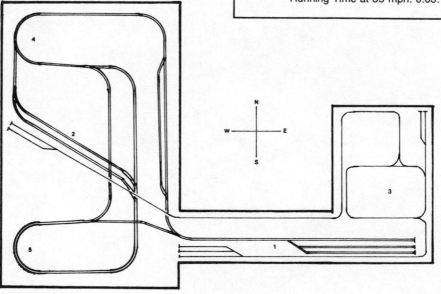

LAYOUT 80

Here is another approach to a combination layout. In this case, the streetcars use some of the tracks that are also used by the railroad. In the center of the layout is the downtown that is served strictly by the streetcars. In order to get to the car barn, these streetcars must travel along tracks that are so used by the railroad as it travels from the railroad station on the west side of the layout to the return loop area on the east side.

In a case like this, consider using suburban one- or two-car electric trains for the railroad portion. That might be more realistic than to run long freight trains in conjunction with the streetcar operation.

Type:	Traction
	Continuous Run

Gauge	Layout in Feet
O	57 x 37
S	43 x 28
OO	36 x 23
HO	31 x 20
TT	23 x 15
N	17 x 11

Track in Feet			
Traction:	120	Railroad:	477
	90		358
	76		300
	66		263
	48		191
	36		143

Turnouts:
  Left Hand: 5
  Right Hand: 5
  Y: 1
  Single Crossover: 1
Crossings: 2
Stations: 2
Return Loops: 2 (Railroad) 1 (Traction)

Traction: Scale Miles: 0.99
          Running Time at 15 mph: 0:03:58
Railroad: Scale Miles: 3.93
          Running Time at 35 mph: 0:06:44

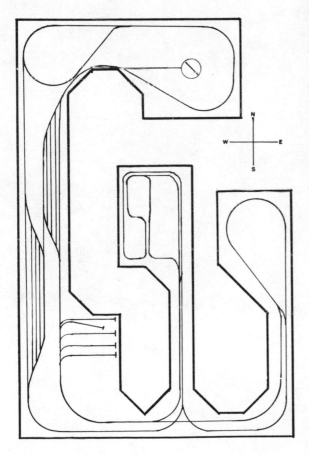

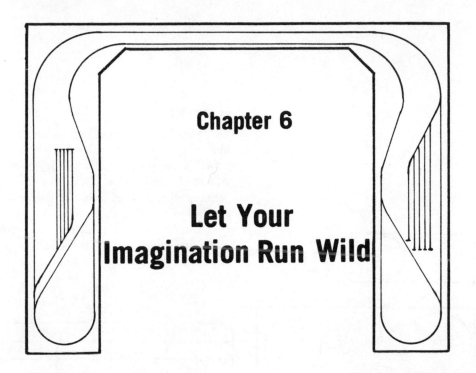

Chapter 6

Let Your
Imagination Run Wild

This chapter contains track-plan suggestions that combine many of the features discussed previously (except traction). Some are fairly simple and some are quite complicated, but there might be an idea here or there that you might be tempted to include in whatever layout you are planning at the moment. Many of these layouts will not necessarily lend themselves to a rigidly structured scheduled operation of the trains. For those who don't care that much about adhering to prototype operation practices, there is likely to be a lot of pleasure available in some of the ideas depicted on the following pages.

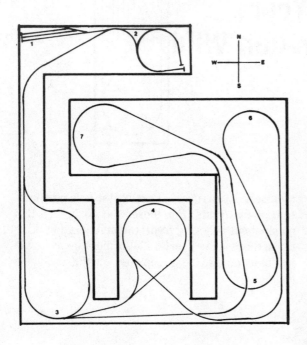

LAYOUT 81

This layout is designed for the modeler who likes to see his or her trains run with a minimum of effort by the operator. Except for a storage area, station (1), and a wye (2), all you have is a long, convoluted main line. Two sections also double as return loops.

This is the type of layout best suited to the creation of landscaping that consists of great mountains, valleys, gorges, and rivers.

Type:	Out and Return	
Gauge	Layout in Feet	Track in Feet
O	40 x 37	337
S	30 x 28	253
OO	25 x 23	212
HO	22 x 20	186
TT	16 x 15	135
N	12 x 11	101

Turnouts	
Left Hand:	4
Right Hand:	1
Three Way:	1
Y:	1
Crossings:	1 (+2)
Stations:	1
Return Loops:	2
Wyes:	1

Scale Miles: 2.78
Running Time at 35 mph: 0:04:46

LAYOUT 82

Figure 6-1 shows a schematic presentation of a part of a city or town where two main lines cross each other at one end of a station. While this, in itself, would not constitute a workable layout, the track can be bent and reconfigured in such a way that it becomes an integral part of a track plan with many operational possibilities.

Figure 6-2 shows one possible solution to that problem. At point 1 is the station that is also identified as 1 in Fig. 6-1. Point 2 is where the two main lines cross in both illustrations. Points 3 and 4 are stations that have been added to provide additional storage space and operational variety.

A train leaving station 3 southbound can make a stop in station 1 and then continue north, east, and south on the far east side of the layout. When turning north once more, it passes again through station 1 and continues on to station 4. Alternately, it can bypass station 4 and enter the second main line that crosses the other at point 2.

Type:	Out and Return Continuous Run	
Gauge	Layout in Feet	Track in Feet
O	67 x 50	513
S	50 x 38	385
OO	42 x 31	323
HO	37 x 28	283
TT	27 x 20	205
N	20 x 15	154

Turnouts
  Left Hand: 1
  Right Hand: 3
  Single Crossover: 2
Crossings: 3 (+2)
Stations: 2
Return Loops: 2

Scale Miles: 4.23
Running Time at 35 mph: 0:07:15

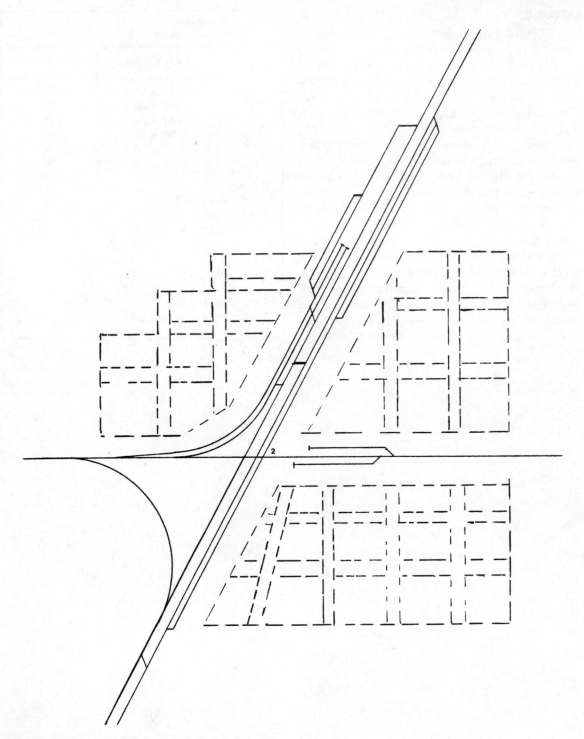

Fig. 6-1. A schematic of the two main lines crossing.

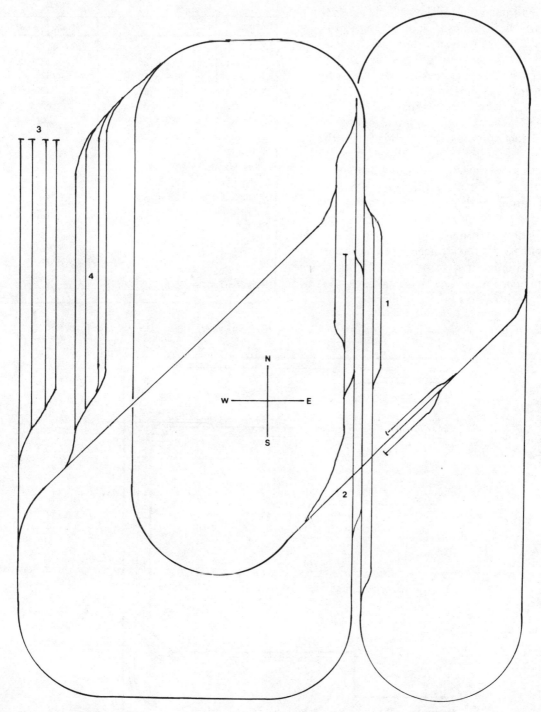

Fig. 6-2. An operational track plan.

LAYOUT 83

This around-the-wall layout is designed to take up relatively little space in an average-size room (assuming use of the smaller scales). It consists of two terminals, two return loops, and a number of parallel main lines that make it possible to operate several trains at one time. See Fig. 6-3.

This is a somewhat simplified version of an N-gauge layout that I built and operated in a 16- × -12 foot room, and that provided me with much pleasure for the three years I lived in that house.

A train leaving station 1 can either go directly to station 2 or it can use the crossover to go into loop 4. From there it has the option of going to either one of the inner main lines. If the center main line is selected, it must move through the double slip switch 3, eventually heading either toward station 5. Alternately, it can use loop 4 to change direction once more and, this time using the third crossover, it can return to station 1.

Type:	Out and Return	
	Continuous Run	
Gauge	Layout in Feet	Track in Feet
O	53 x 33	417
S	40 x 25	313
OO	34 x 21	262
HO	29 x 18	230
TT	21 x 13	167
N	16 x 10	125

Turnouts:
Left Hand: 2
Right Hand: 5
Single Crossover: 3
Slip Switch: 1
Stations: 2
Return Loops: 2

Scale Miles: 3.44
Running Time at 35 mph: 0:05:53

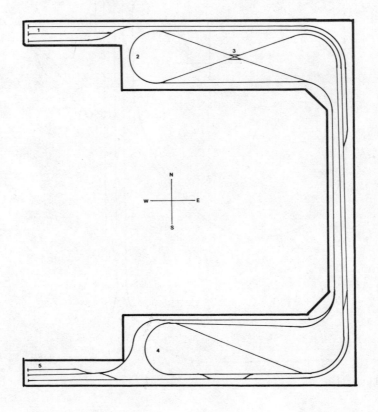

Fig. 6-3. A narrow shelf built along a windowsill can serve to connect two portions of a layout located on opposite sides of the room.

LAYOUT 84

Here is a two-level layout. One portion can be completely beneath the other or possibly offset by a foot or so. Figure 6-4 shows two stations that should probably be on the upper level. The switching operations associated with stations and terminals tend to require frequent access by the operator. The north-south track between the two stations is there to provide the possibility of having a train run continuously.

At points 3 and 4, the track leads from the upper to the lower level and vice versa. The portion of the layout shown in Fig. 6-5 consists of the main line, a return loop (7), and a wye (6). Using both levels, trains can run continuously or they can shuttle between stations in either direction.

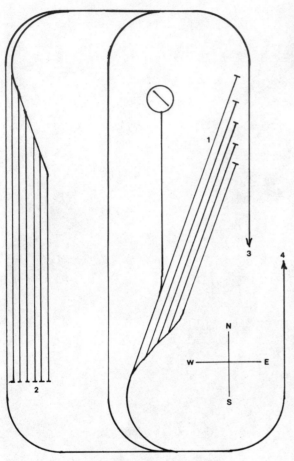

Fig. 6-4. A layout with two upper-level stations.

Type:	Out and Return	
	Continuous Run	

Gauge	Layout in Feet	Track in Feet
O	23 x 15	220
S	18 x 11	165
OO	15 x 9	139
HO	13 x 8	121
TT	9 x 6	88
N	7 x 4.5	66

Turnouts
  Left Hand: 5
  Right Hand: 4
Stations: 2
Return Loops: 1
Wyes: 1

Scale Miles: 1.81
Running Time at 35 mph: 0:03:07

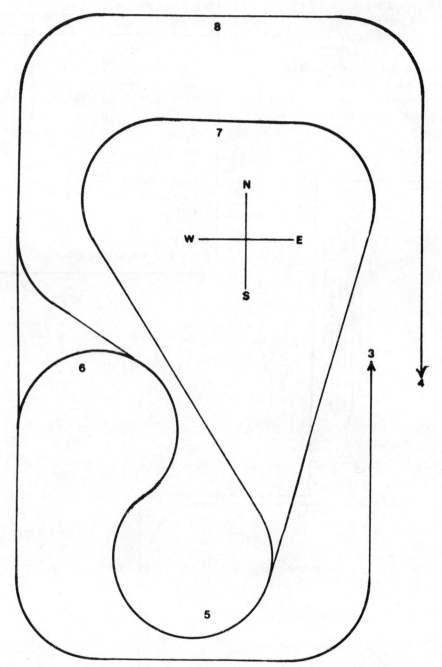

Fig. 6-5. A main line, a return loop, and a wye.

LAYOUT 85

Here is a layout somewhat similar to the ones shown in Figs. 6-4 and 6-5. Here the two stations and the main line are all on one level. This layout has no return loops or wyes. Anyone actually building a version of it might be well advised to add the turnouts and sections of track that would be needed to provide a means to reverse the direction of travel. One simple solution would be to eliminate the overpass and replace it with a double slip switch.

Type:	Out and Return Continuous Run	
Gauge	Layout in Feet	Track in Feet
O	30 x 20	127
S	23 x 15	95
OO	19 x 13	80
HO	17 x 11	70
TT	12 x 8	51
N	9 x 6	38

Turnouts
  Left Hand: 2
  Right Hand: 4
  Single Crossover: 1
Crossings: 0 (1)
Stations: 2

Scale Miles: 1.04
Running Time at 35 mph: 0:01:47

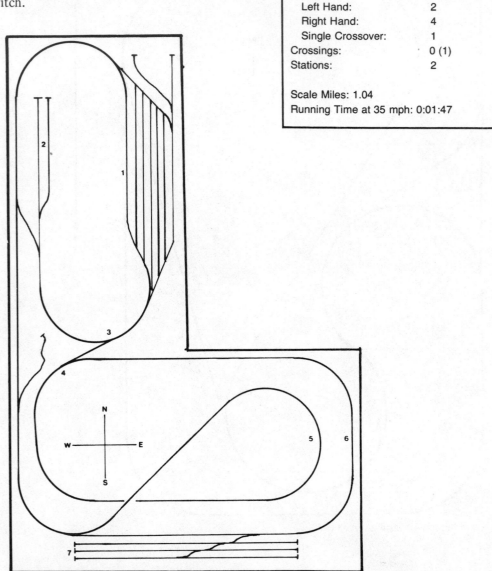

LAYOUT 86

This layout might fit into a basement area around furnaces and other such obstacles. It consists of two stations and fairly long sections of main line. Three sections of the main line are return loops (3, 5, and 6).

The fascinating feature about this layout, in terms of operation, would be an attempt to run two trains simultaneously. Both trains would have to use the same sections of the main line for travel in either direction. This would keep one or more operators very attentive.

If multiple train operation is to be performed with any degree of frequency, it would probably be a good idea to consider adding one or even two passing sidings along certain stretches of the main line.

Type:	Out and Return Continuous Run	
Gauge	Layout in Feet	Track in Feet
O	30 x 20	237
S	23 x 15	178
OO	19 x 13	149
HO	17 x 11	130
TT	12 x 8	95
N	9 x 6	71

Turnouts
  Left Hand: 2
  Right Hand: 4
Crossings: 2 (+4)
Stations: 2
Return Loops: 3

Scale Miles: 1.95
Running Time at 35 mph: 0:03:21

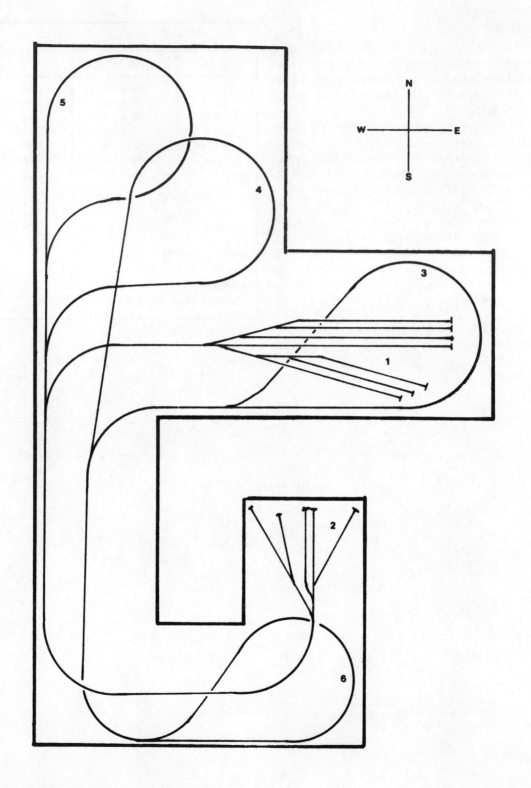

LAYOUT 87

This track plan concentrates much of the available space on two stations or terminals. It provides ample opportunity for switching operations (depending on the way the tracks in the stations are laid out). The rest of the space is used for a relatively short main line that also incorporates two return loops (3 and 6).

Type:	Out and Return Continuous Run	
Gauge	Layout in Feet	Track in Feet
O	23 x 17	103
S	18 x 13	78
OO	15 x 10	65
HO	13 x 9	57
TT	9 x 7	41
N	7 x 5	31

Turnouts
   Left Hand: 4
   Right Hand: 3
Crossings: 1 (+2)
Stations: 2
Return Loops: 2

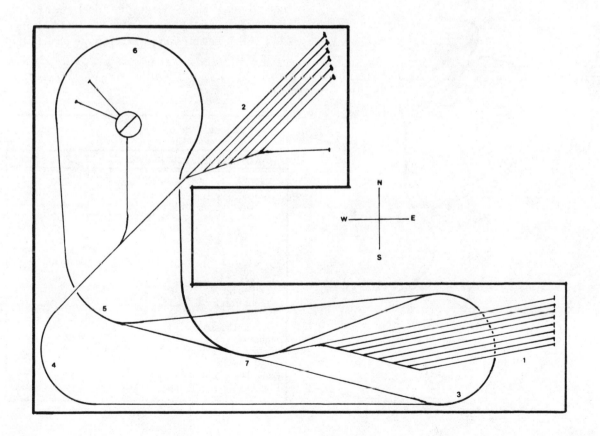

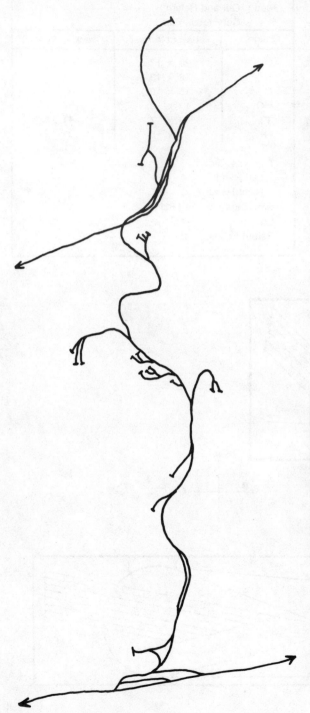

LAYOUT 88

Figure 6-6 shows a diagram of an actual track that connects two main lines. By using this basic track plan and by connecting the two main lines, turning them into one, it can become the basis for an interesting layout.

Figure 6-7 is a schematic representation of that same section of track. This kind of intermediate step in layout planning—when you are trying to use a certain section of prototype as the basis for our layout—is useful in providing a somewhat clearer picture of what is involved.

Figure 6-8 is one solution for an actual layout that incorporates most of the spurs, passing sidings, and so on. It allows for a great deal of switching operations, and there are two wyes (near points 6 and 7) that permit you to reverse the direction of train travel.

Type:	Out and Return Continuous Run	
Gauge	Layout in Feet	Track in Feet
O	60 x 47	330
S	45 x 35	248
OO	38 x 29	208
HO	33 x 26	182
TT	24 x 19	132
N	18 x 14	99

Turnouts
  Left Hand: 6
  Right Hand: 7
  Y: 4
  Single Crossover: 1
Stations: 3
Wyes: 2

Scale Miles: 2.72
Running Time at 35 mph: 0:04:40

Fig. 6-6. A track diagram.

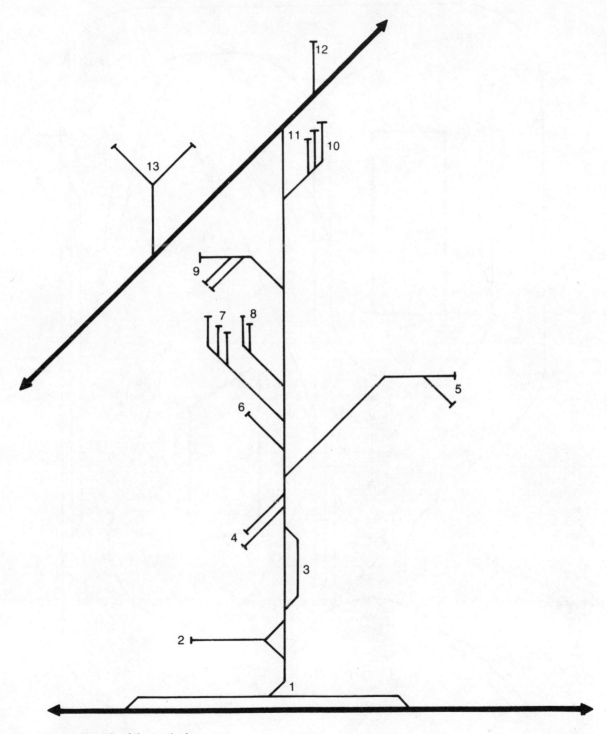

Fig. 6-7. A schematic of the track plan.

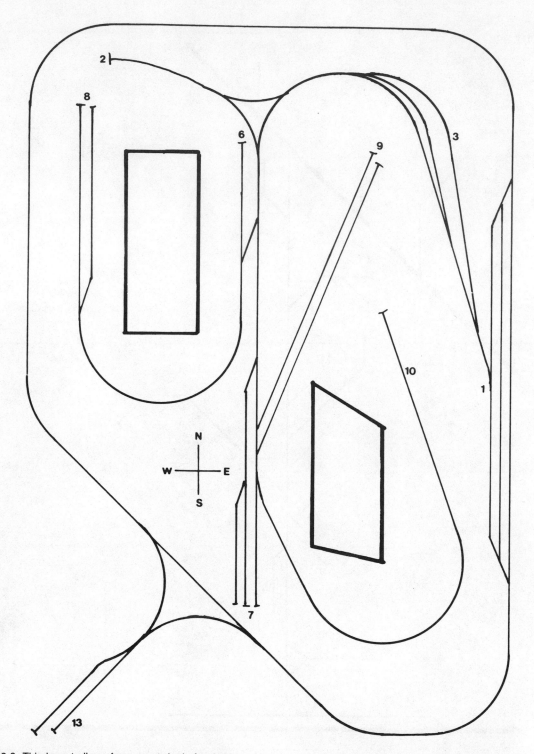

Fig. 6-8. This layout allows for a great deal of switching.

LAYOUT 89

Here three stations (1, 2, and 3) are connected by a main line consisting, for all practical purposes, of two ovals. No provision is made for reversing the direction of train travel. Nevertheless, adding such a possibility would not be too difficult.

Type:	Out and Return	
	Continuous Run	
Gauge	Layout in Feet	Track in Feet
O	50 x 37	343
S	38 x 28	258
OO	31 x 23	216
HO	28 x 20	189
TT	20 x 15	137
N	15 x 11	103

Turnouts
  Left Hand: 3
  Right Hand: 8
Crossings: 3
Stations: 3

Scale Miles: 2.83
Running Time at 35 mph: 0:04:51

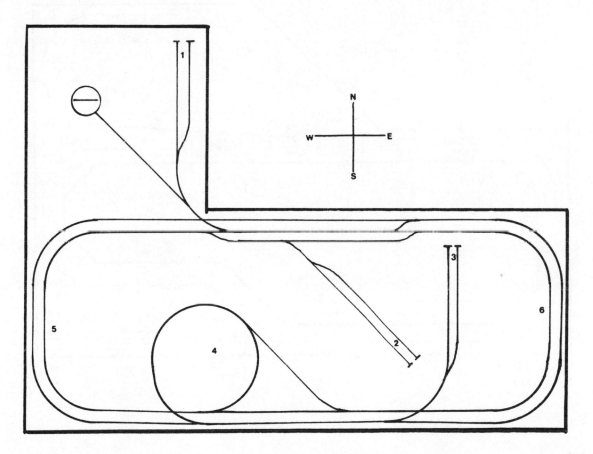

LAYOUT 90

This layout consists of one terminal and one station or freight yard. It depends on how the modeler wants to use the undeveloped area at the southeast corner of the layout. One main line connects the two stations directly while another consists of an oval, including a passing siding. The two are connected with a double crossover. Except for the circular section of track (2), no provision has been made for reversing the direction of train travel.

Type:	Out and Return Continuous Run	
Gauge	Layout in Feet	Track in Feet
O	28 x 18	177
S	21 x 14	133
OO	17 x 12	111
HO	16 x 10	97
TT	11 x 7	71
N	8.5 x 5.5	53

Turnouts
  Left Hand: 4
  Right Hand: 3
  Double Crossover: 1
Stations: 2
Return Loops: 1

Scale Miles: 1.46
Running Time at 35 mph: 0:02:30

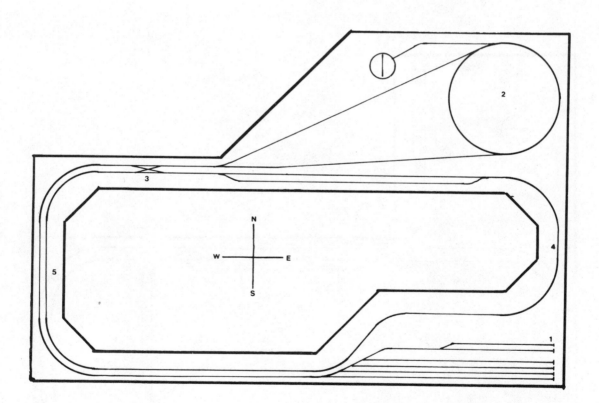

LAYOUT 91

This is another case where I have diagramed a prototype section of track. This one is located in northern Washington and southern British Columbia. Figure 6-9 shows a fairly true representation of the actual tracks.

Figure 6-10 reduces the actual track plan to a schematic representation. This makes it easier to try to figure out a way to bend the whole thing like a bunch of pretzels in order to fit it into whatever space is available for your layout.

Figure 6-11 shows the result of that bending operation. The various numbers and letters correspond to the stations and track section on the prototype and schematic plans. The layout does permit continuous operation, but it is best suited for operation of several trains that are controlled by several operators using cab control. No provision has been made to reverse the direction of train travel.

Type:	Out and Return Continuous Run	
Gauge	Layout in Feet	Track in Feet
O	28 x 18	240
S	21 x 14	180
OO	18 x 12	151
HO	17 x 10	132
TT	11 x 7	96
N	8.5 x 5.5	72

Turnouts
Left Hand: 8
Right Hand: 11
Y: 1
Crossings: 0 (2)
Stations: 11

Scale Miles: 1.98
Running Time at 35 mph: 0:03:24

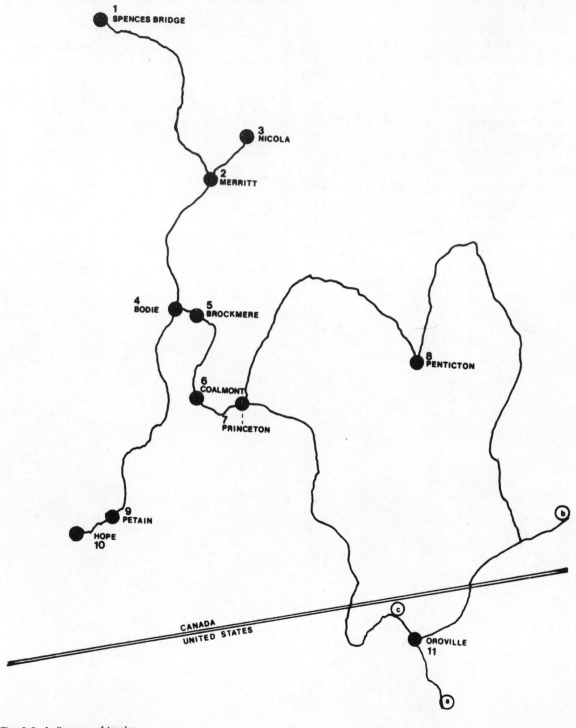

Fig. 6-9. A diagram of tracks.

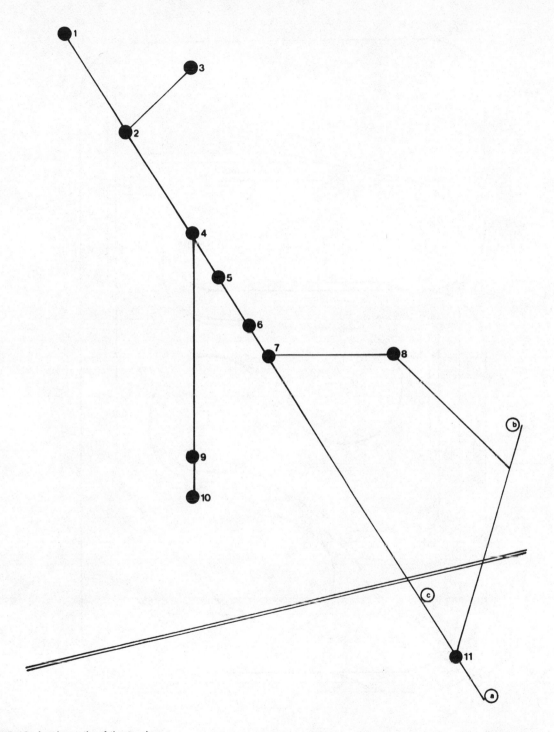

Fig. 6-10. A schematic of the tracks.

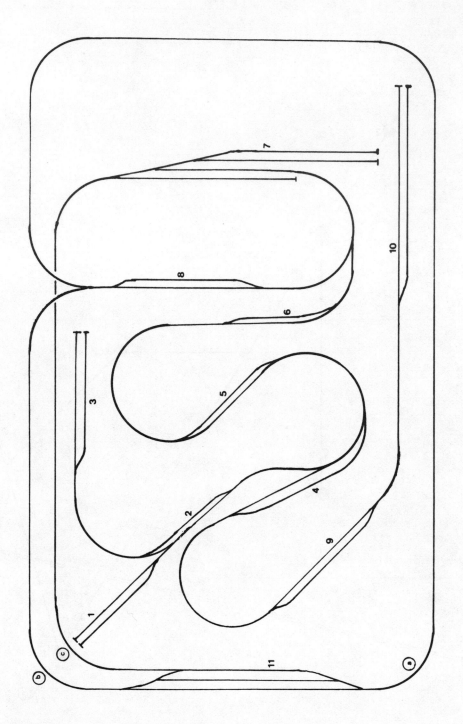

Fig. 6-11. This layout is best suited for operating several trains.

LAYOUT 92

Here one area of a layout is used to accommodate three stations that should be separated from each other by some type of landscaping device. The advantage of having all three in more or less the same area is that one operator can deal with all of them. The rest of the layout is used for the main line. Included is one return loop. Passing sidings and spurs can be added at your discretion.

Type:	Out and Return Continuous Run	
Gauge	Layout in Feet	Track in Feet
O	27 x 18	173
S	20 x 14	130
OO	17 x 11.5	109
HO	15 x 10	96
TT	11 x 7	69
N	8 x 5.5	52

Turnouts
  Left Hand: 2
  Right Hand: 2
Crossings: 0 (4)
Stations: 2
Return Loops: 1

Scale Miles :1.43
Running Time at 35 mph: 0:02:27

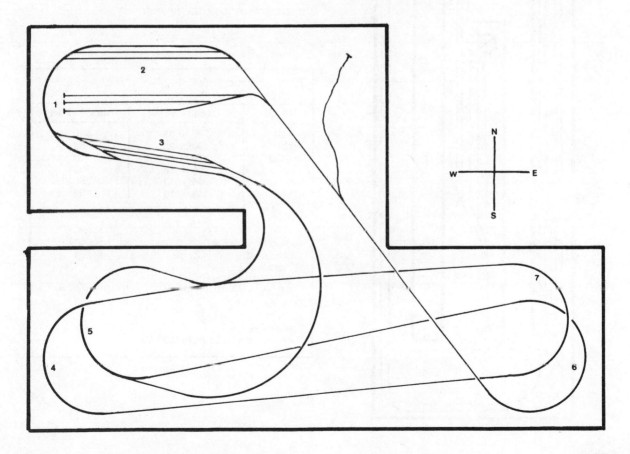

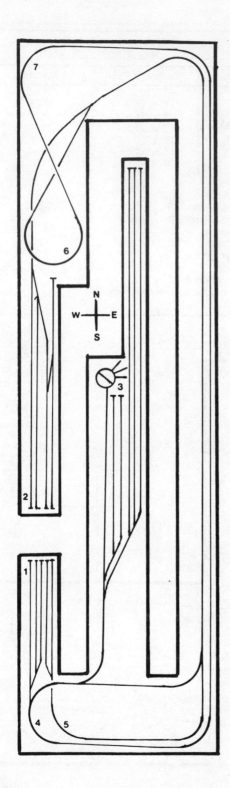

LAYOUT 93

Here is a long and narrow layout that could be placed against the back wall of a garage if the cars you are driving are short. At first glance, it looks as if there are just three stations. There are actually four stations because tracks 4 and 5 lead to separate portions of the station marked 1. If those two station sections are separated by some type of structure or landscaping device, they would become independent units.

No return loops or wyes are included. Nevertheless, it would be possible to provide for the reversal of train travel by placing either a double crossover or two opposing single crossovers between the two north-south main-line sections on the far-east side of the layout.

Type:	Out and Return	
	Continuous Run	

Gauge	Layout in Feet	Track in Feet
O	120 x 33	640
S	90 x 25	480
OO	76 x 21	403
HO	66 x 18	353
TT	48 x 13	256
N	36 x 10	192

Turnouts
Left Hand: 2
Right Hand: 1
Single Crossover: 1
Crossings: 0 (4)
Stations: 4

Scale Miles: 5.28
Running Time at 35 mph: 0:09:03

LAYOUT 94

This layout could represent one, two, or three stations. Point 1 represents a terminal. Point 2 could be a station along the mainline. Point 8 could be a freight yard or another station. The balance of the layout consists of enough main line to operate more than one train at a time. Also included are two return loops. See Fig. 6-12.

Type:	Out and Return Continuous Run	
Gauge	Layout in Feet	Track in Feet
O	60 x 37	543
S	45 x 38	408
OO	38 x 23	342
HO	33 x 20	299
TT	24 x 15	217
N	18 x 11	163

Turnouts
  Left Hand: 7
  Right Hand: 4
  Single Crossover: 2
Crossings: 0 (4)
Stations: 3
Return Loops: 2

Scale Miles: 4.48
Running Time at 35 mph: 0:07:41

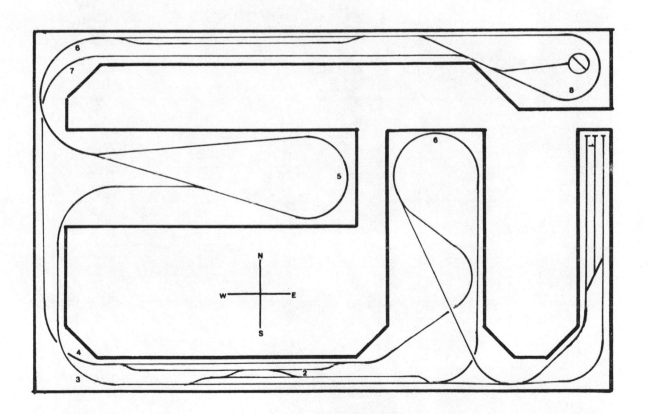

Fig. 6-12. A busy moment on the layout.

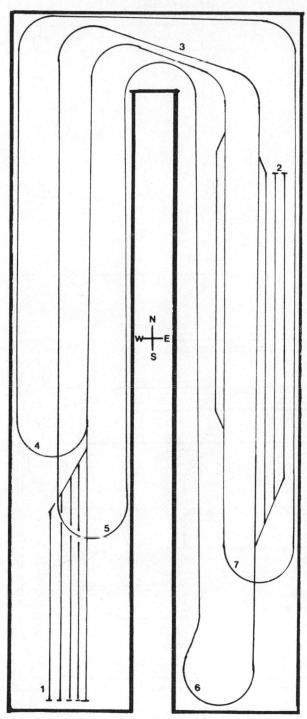

LAYOUT 95

Here are actually two entirely separate main lines and trains leaving from either station in either direction. They will be able to continue to travel without ever being able to get onto the other section of the main line. This could be useful in a situation where two different gauges or standard and narrow gauge are being used.

If that is not the case, the double crossover at point 3 would solve the problem of getting a train traveling on the main line, identified by loops 4 and 7, to move over to the main line identified as 5 and 6.

Type:	Out and Return Continuous Run	
Gauge	Layout in Feet	Track in Feet
O	57 x 37	463
S	43 x 28	348
OO	36 x 23	292
HO	31 x 20	255
TT	23 x 15	185
N	17 x 7	139

Turnouts
  Left Hand: 2
Right Hand: 3
Double Crossover: 1 (optional)
Crossings: 2 (+1)
Stations: 2
Return Loops: 0 (2 if double crossover is installed)

Scale Miles: 3.82
Running Time at 35 mph: 0:06:33

LAYOUT 96

This is something for the fairly ambitious modeler who either owns the space in which the layout is to be built or at least has a very long lease. There are three stations and a confusing maze of main line that includes one return loop. Depending on how the turnouts are operated, this layout permits great variety in terms of train travel. See Fig. 6-13.

Assuming that more than one person is available to control the operation of individual trains, it would seem to me that three or even four trains could easily be operated at the same time.

Type:	Out and Return Continuous Run	
Gauge	Layout in Feet	Track in Feet
O	54 x 33	1,303
S	40 x 25	978
OO	34 x 21	821
HO	29 x 18	718
TT	21 x 13	521
N	16 x 10	391

Turnouts
 Left Hand: 5
 Right Hand: 4
 Single Crossover: 2
Crossings: 0 (11)
Stations: 3
Return Loops: 1

Scale Miles: 10.75
Running Time at 35 mph: 0:18:26

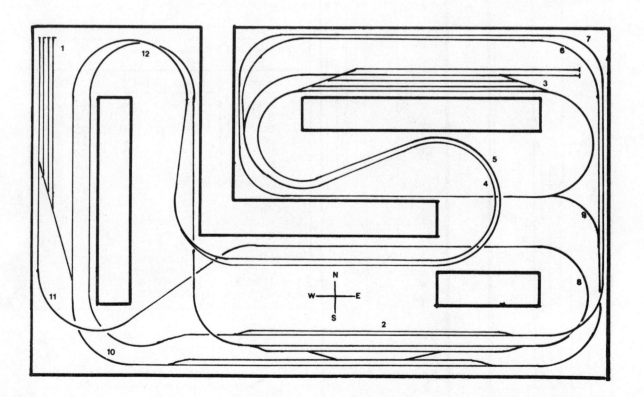

Fig. 6-13. Here two trains are operating simultaneously, but independent of each other.

LAYOUT 97

Here is a bunch of stations, four in all, and some rather convoluted main line that includes one return loop. While the continuous running of one or two trains is possible, the layout lends itself better to point-to-point operation. A number of trains can be used at the same time; each is controlled by a separate operator.

The return loop is fairly hard to find, but a train moving southeastward at point 5 will eventually return to that same turnout in the opposite direction.

Type:	Out and Return	
	Continuous Run	

Gauge	Layout in Feet	Track in Feet
O	93 x 73	1,113
S	70 x 55	835
OO	59 x 46	701
HO	51 x 40	614
TT	37 x 29	445
N	28 x 22	334

Turnouts
  Left Hand: 7
  Right Hand: 6
  Single Crossover: 4
Crossings: 1 (+10)
Stations: 4
Return Loops: 1

Scale Miles: 9.18
Running Time at 35 mph: 0:15:44

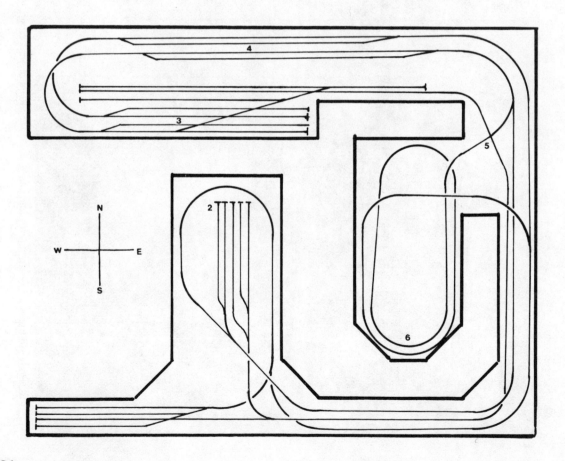

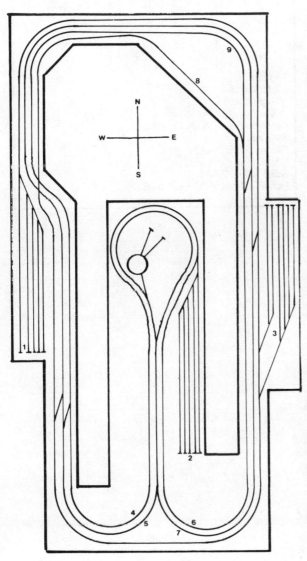

LAYOUT 98

Three stations and a lot of main line, including one return loop, compose this layout. The operational possibilities are not immediately apparent until you follow a train from place to place and use the crossovers in order to get from one part of the main line to another.

At least three trains, possibly more, could easily operate simultaneously on this layout. Keeping them out of each other's way would be the fun of it.

| Type: | Out and Return | |
| | Continuous Run | |

Gauge	Layout in Feet	Track in Feet
O	57 x 30	587
S	43 x 23	440
OO	36 x 19	370
HO	31 x 17	323
TT	23 x 12	235
N	17 x 9	176

Turnouts
  Right Hand: 1
  Y: 2
  Single Crossover: 4
Crossings: 2
Stations: 3
Return Loops: 1

Scale Miles: 4.84
Running Time at 35 mph: 0:08:18

LAYOUT 99

This layout might be useful when there are two areas that are separated by a long, narrow space. An example is two separate rooms at either end of a hallway. What you have is one station and one industrial or mine area with several spurs. The two are connected by a long section of main line that includes a return loop at 2 and another going from the double slip switch at 3 to the loop at 4.

Depending on the width of the space available in the long and narrow section, one or two passing sidings could be added to permit the operation of several trains in opposite directions.

Type:	Out and Return	
	Continuous Run	

Gauge	Layout in Feet	Track in Feet
O	83 x 57	360
S	63 x 43	270
OO	52 x 36	227
HO	46 x 31	198
TT	33 x 23	144
N	25 x 17	108

Turnouts
Left Hand: 2
Right Hand: 2
Slip Switch: 1
Crossings: 0 (2)
Stations: 1
Return Loops: 2

Scale Miles: 2.97
Running Time at 35 mph: 0:05:05

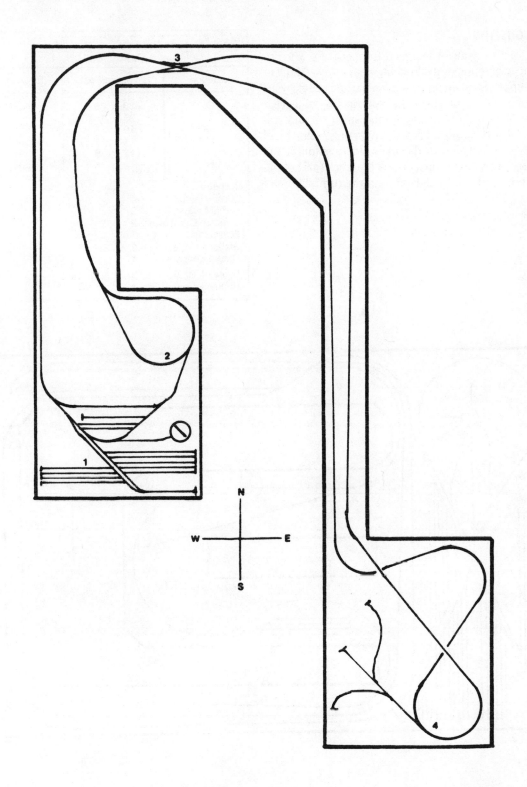

LAYOUT 100

This layout is designed for modelers who delight in complicated switching operations. Much of the space is taken up by a terminal and freight yard combination. The rest consists primarily of a great deal of main line, including one small second station. There is no means of reversing train-travel direction included in the main line portion of the layout. The only return loop is the track (part of the freight yard) that winds around the turntable.

Type:	Out and Return Continuous Run	
Gauge	Layout in Feet	Track in Feet
O	30 x 20	380
S	23 x 15	285
OO	19 x 13	239
HO	17 x 11	209
TT	12 x 8	152
N	9 x 6	114

Turnouts
  Left Hand: 4
  Right Hand: 3
  Single Crossover: 2
Crossings: 0 (2)
Stations: 2
Return Loops: 1

Scale Miles: 3.13
Running Time at 35 mph: 0:05:22

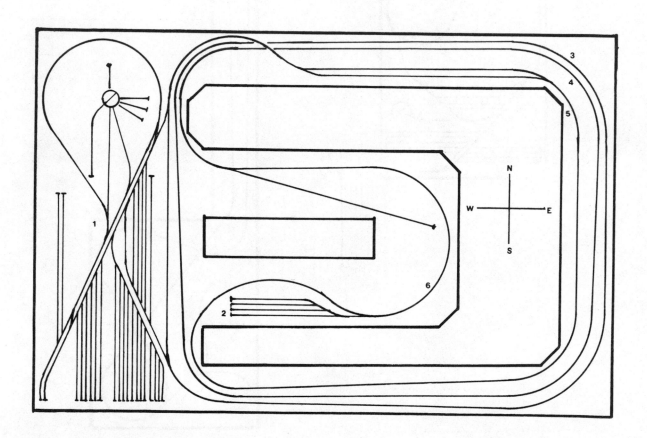

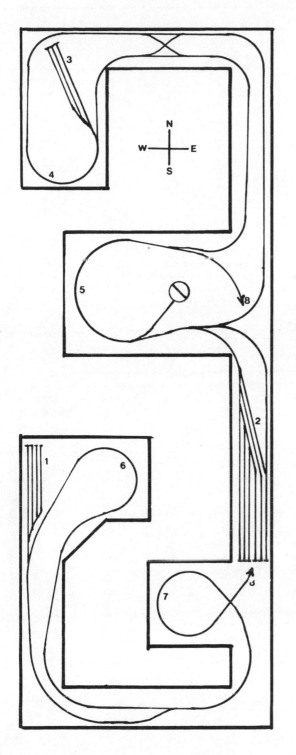

LAYOUT 101

Here are three stations and a main line that incorporate two return loops. Because station 2 takes up all the available space in that area, to connect the two points marked 8 on the layout, you will have to either drop the main line below the level of station 2 or climb it above.

Type:	Out and Return	
	Continuous Run	

Gauge	Layout in Feet	Track in Feet
O	83 x 30	593
S	63 x 23	445
OO	52 x 19	374
HO	46 x 17	327
TT	33 x 12	237
N	25 x 9	178

Turnouts
  Left Hand: 4
  Right Hand: 2
  Y: 1
  Double Crossover: 1
Crossings: 1
Stations: 3
Return Loops: 2

Scale Miles: 4.89
Running Time at 35 mph: 0:08:23

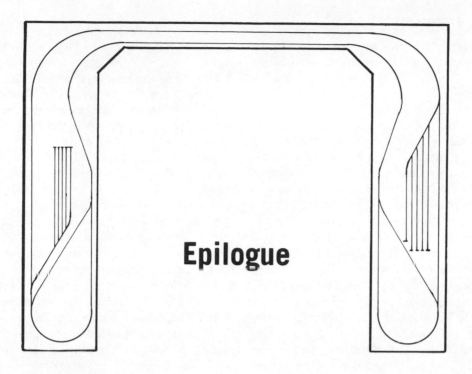

Epilogue

Now comes the hard part; the actual building of the layout, the laying of track, and so on. Although this is a book of layout concepts, I would feel amiss if I didn't add a few words on the techniques.

Any model railroad layout consists basically of three parts: the base or benchwork, the actual tracks, and the landscaping. Electrical systems are really a separate issue.

The *substructure*, the base on which the layout will eventually be built, can be simply a large piece of plywood, a slab door, or any other solid sheet that can accept spikes and nails without too much difficulty. Most novice modelers are likely to construct their first layout on such a solid base simply because it appears, at first glance, to be the easiest and fastest way to get going.

You will find out later—after drilling a million holes to provide access for the electrical wiring and when you realize that it is difficult, if not impossible, to drop the elevation of a track below the average ground level of the layout—that the drawbacks of such a solid base become apparent.

Most advanced modelers opt for what is known as *benchwork*. This type of open-grid construction supports narrow strips of plywood or other roadbed wherever the tracks will be laid. Most model railroad magazines delight in publishing illustrated articles that show, with the precision of an architect, how such benchwork should be constructed, what size wood should be used, and so on. That's all a bunch of nonsense.

Anyone able to drive a nail or wield a screwdriver can build perfectly adequate benchwork out of a collection of scrap lumber. Since most or all of it will eventually be hidden from view, neatness is really of no consequence. Just make sure that it is sturdy and that it doesn't shake or wobble.

Once the base for the layout has been decided upon and constructed, the next step involves the actual laying of the tracks. Some perfectionists might insist on laying individual rails on separate ties (striving for the last word in realism). When this is well done it looks great, but the work involved is monstrous.

If this degree of realism seems important, it should probably be restricted to the areas of the layout that are right in front of the eyes of the observer. It would seem to be a case of gilding the lily to use this type of technique in places that will eventually be hidden from view.

Another technique, available in some scales, is a wooden base called TrueScale. This consists of milled ties on a solid wooden base and it makes laying tracks considerably simpler. This roadbed comes in straight and curved sections. Some sections are cut into at regular intervals on either side to permit a degree of flexibility. Track laid in this manner looks acceptably realistic. Assuming a reasonable degree of care is taken, it automatically assures that the space between rails is constant.

The simplest solution involves the use of Flex-track; rails are fastened to a flexible base of plastic ties. This track can be laid quite quickly. The space between rails is assured, and the track can be bent into any kind of curve that might be required. It can be fastened to the base with brads pushed through holes provided in the center of the ties or it can be glued down. In that case, any subsequent change becomes quite difficult. At first glance, this technique appears to provide the least realistic result. Nevertheless, it can subsequently be dressed up with gravel, sand, and what have you to look perfectly acceptable.

I used TrueScale in the days when I built my layouts in HO gauge, but I switched to Flextrack once I decided on N-gauge. It is easier to deal with and it is by far the least expensive method of building a track plan that involves a lot of tracks.

And then there is the landscaping, the scenery and structures that eventually transform your layout from a naked skeleton into a thing of beauty. Landscaping a layout is usually a never-ending task. There is always one more detail to be added or some small improvement that might add realism to one corner of the layout or another.

The importance of landscaping cannot be overemphasized. The beauty and artistry of the final design—if there ever is a really *final* design—is limited only by your imagination and patience. A good practice is to look at the whole as a collection of small scenes. Complete one small section at a time and then go on to the next. That way the final design is more likely to have a distinctive character, rather than being a hodgepodge of unrelated mountains and valleys.

Whatever you do, take your time with every phase of layout design, construction, and finishing. Small mistakes and a bit of sloppiness here and there tend to be the breeders of hours of aggravation. If everything is done with care from the very beginning, there can be no doubt that model railroading is a great deal of fun.

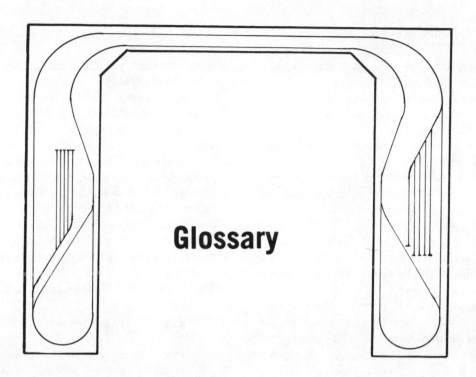

Glossary

abutment—The foundation or structure supporting the ends of a bridge, often including the retaining walls which are part of the approaches.

ac—*See* alternating current.

alternating current—Electrical current which reverses its polarity at regular intervals or cycles expressed at Hz (Hertz). Thus 60 Hz = 60 cycles per second.

ampere—A measurement for the volume rather than the force of electrical current. Technically, the unit of current flowing through 1 ohm resistance at 1 volt potential in 1 second. Usually expressed in the abbreviated form: amp.

articulated—Describes steam engines powered by several engines driving several groups of driving wheels. The usual configurations are 2-6-6-2, 4-6-6-4, 2-8-8-2, or 4-8-8-4.

ballast—Gravel, crushed rock, stone, or similar material placed around the ties to provide support and adequate drainage.

benchwork—Any type of permanent support for a model railroad layout. It can consist of open grids or a solid board supported by legs.

block—A section of track which, in prototype operation, is controlled by signals; in model railroading it is a section of the track controlled by separate speed and directional controls.

block control—The system of dividing the control of a model railroad layout into individual blocks.

bridge rectifier—Four arms in a diamond-shaped arrangement employing four simple diodes to provide full-wave rectification of an ac power supply.

cab—The part of a locomotive occupied by the controls and housing the engineer. In model railroading, an electrical control unit for the control of speed and direction on a layout operated under the principle of cab control.

cab control—A method which permits one operator to control a specific engine independently of others operating simultaneously on different blocks.

cab forward—A type of steam engine where the cab is in the front.

caboose—A special car carrying the crew of a freight train and always coupled to the extreme rear of the train.

camelback—A steam engine with the cab astride the boiler.

catenary—The overhead trolley-wire system used by trolley cars and other electrical rolling stock.

center pin—*See* kingpin.

circumference—The total distance around the outer perimeter of a circle. It always measures the radius multiplied by 3.1415926, in mathematics known as π (pi).

common rail—A rail, the electrical continuity of which is maintained through several blocks.

common return—The electrical connection between a power source and a device which does not include any kind of controls.

compass (draftsman's)—A tool used in drawing circles.

contacts—The points at which conductors touch to produce electrical current flow.

control rail—The gapped rail used for block control when several blocks share a common rail.

crossing—An intersection of two railroad tracks or of a railroad track and a road or highway.

crossing gate—A moving bar which is lowered to protect the track upon the approach of a train.

crossover—A two-turnout arrangement providing a connection between two parallel tracks.

dc—*See* direct current.

detailing—Refining a model, scenery, landscaping etc.

diameter—The measurement from one side of a circle through the center to the other side. It is twice the radius.

diode—A component consisting of two electrodes: one cathode and one anode. It is used in model railroading as a component of a rectifier.

diorama—A three-dimensional scene, usually with no moving parts.

direct current—Electrical current which flows in one direction only.

double crossover—*See* scissors crossover. Also, simply two ordinary crossovers with the turnouts arranged in opposite directions.

double-pole double-throw switch—An electrical switch which permits the connection of two separate currents each to one of two contacts. In model railroading it is used to reverse the direction of the current energizing the track.

double-pole single-throw switch—An electric switch which permits the connection or disconnection of two separate currents to or from one contact.

DPDT switch—Double-pole double-throw switch.

DPST switch—Double-pole single-throw switch.

elevation—The distance between the base level of the layout and the level of elevated track, usually expressed in scale feet.

flange—The vertical extension on the inside of a wheel, designed to keep the wheels on the track.

frog—The juncture point of the inside rails in a turnout.

gage—*See* gauge.

gauge—The distance between the inside of the railhead of the two rails which make up the track.

grab-iron—The handholds on freight cars used to climb to the roof of the car.

grade—The degree that a section of track either rises or falls.

guard rails—Rails placed inside the running rails in turnouts, crossings, bridges, trestles, etc. to reduce the chances for derailment.

HO-gauge—One inch equals 87.1 inches.

hump—A section of elevation rail at one end of a classification yard. Cars can be cut loose to roll onto the appropriate yard track by gravity.

humpyard—A classification yard equipped with a hump rail.

independent block system—A system of block control in which no two blocks have a common rail.

kingpin—The pin holding the truck to the bottom of the car.

"kitbash"—A unique model railroad expression referring to the use of parts from one or several kits in the construction of something other than that for which the kits were intended.

ladder track—A series of turnouts, as are usually found in a freight yard.

layout—The model railroad setup constructed on a permanent base. Also often referred to as pike.

lichen—A flowerless, moss-like plant growing primarily on the surface of rocks. In preserved form it is a favorite means of creating model vegetation.

mainline—The track between stations.

momentary contact switch—A normally open switch which makes contact only while it is being operated, such as an ordinary push button.

narrow gauge—In prototype, a track with a gauge of less than 4 foot 8½ inches. In modeling, a track which represents such narrow-gauge track, usually referred to as O_{n3} (in O-gauge) or HO_{n3} (in HO-gauge).

N-gauge—One inch equals 160 inches.

nichrome—A conducting wire which glows and stretches when electricity is passed through it, causing it to heat.

NMRA—National Model Railroad Association.

normally closed switch—An electrical switch in which the contact is always made except when the switch is operated.

normally open switch—A switch in which no contact is made except when it is being operated.

O-gauge—One inch equals 48 inches.

Ohm—A measure of electrical resistance. Technically, the resistance across which 1 volt will cause a current of 1 amp to flow.

OO-gauge—One inch equals 76.2 inches.

pantograph—The current pickup on electrical engines, a more or less diamond-shaped arrangement.

piggyback—The carriage of truck trailers on flat cars.

pike—*See* layout.

points (turnout)—The moving rail section of a turnout.

power pack—Term applied to a combination transformer, rectifier, and rheostat. Usually also a means of reversing the flow of the dc current.

prototype—The real world.

pulse power—The type of direct current resulting from the use of a half-wave rectifier. It is particularly helpful in running model trains at very low speeds, or on dirty track.

radius—The distance from the center of a circle to its periphery.

rail—Slang for a person working on the railroad and for a model railroader.

railhead—The top section of the rail on which the wheels run.

rectifier—Equipment used to change alternating current to direct current.

reefer—Refrigerator car.

relay—An electrical switch operated by remote control, usually using a solenoid.

return loop—Any portion of track which causes the train to reverse direction of travel.

rheostat—A resistor the value of which is adjustable. Rheostats are used in model railroading to control the speed of the engines.

right of way—The track, roadbed, and area surrounding the track which is property of the railroad company.

rolling stock—Cars, engines, anything that moves on the track.

roundhouse—A storage and maintenance facility for engines built around a turntable with the stub rails from the turntable leading into its individual stalls.

scale—The proportion between prototype and the model.

scenery—Everything on a model railroad layout other than track, control devices, rolling stock, and other items related directly to the operation of the railroad.

scissors crossover—Two crossovers in opposite direction with a crossing in the center, used primarily to conserve space.

scratch-building—Building a model from basic materials without the use of a kit.

searchlight signal—A light signal with a single light source. The color is changed through the use of filters.

semaphore—A type of signal using moving arms plus lights to indicate the condition of the track ahead.

S-gauge—One inch equals 64 inches.

shay—A type of geared steam locomotive used primarily in mining and logging operations. Its cylinders are mounted vertically on the side of the boiler.

siding—A track running parallel to a section of the mainline to permit trains to pass one another.

signals—Any type of equipment used to indicate the condition of the track ahead, and to control the movement of trains.

single-pole double-throw switch—An electrical switch in which one pole can be connected to either one of two contacts.

single-pole single-throw switch—An electrical switch in which one pole and one contact can be either connected or disconnected.

slab door—A plain door consisting of thin sheets of plywood on both sides. It is hollow on the inside. All slab doors are 6 feet 8½ inches in length and come in many different widths.

slip switch—A rather complicated combination of four turnouts and a crossing serving a purpose similar to that accomplished by a scissors crossover, but using still less space. There are single and double slip switches.

solenoid—An electromagnet.

SPDT switch—Single-pole double-throw switch.

spring switch—A turnout, the points of which are held in one position by a spring so that all trains entering the turnout from the leading side will always move the same way. Trains entering from the trailing side can move through the turnout from either track.

SPST switch—Single-pole single-throw switch.

spur—A dead-end section of track, connected to other track at one end only.

switch machine—Any device, usually electrical, used to operate turnouts by remote control.

switch points—The movable sections of rail in a turnout.

tender—The car used to carry coal and water for steam engines.

tinplate—A term used to denote toy trains. It stems from when the rails of old-style toy trains were manufactured from bent tin.

track—Two rails and the ties which hold them in place.

traction—Trolley cars or any other electrically operated rolling stock obtaining its power from overhead wires.

transformer—A piece of equipment designed to transform current of one voltage to current of another voltage.

trolley—Electrically operated cars used in urban transportation. Also, the pole which rides up against the overhead wire, picking up the current.

TrueScale—A trade name for wooden roadbed to which rails can be spiked with relative ease.

TT-gauge—One inch equals 120 inches or 10 feet.

turnout—Any track switch.

turntable—A rotating platform or bridge with a section of track, used to turn locomotives.

wye—A Y-shaped section of track, often used to make it possible to turn engines around. It usually takes up less space than a return loop.

wig-wag—A warning signal used at road and highway crossings.

Z-gauge—One inch equals 220 inches.

Index

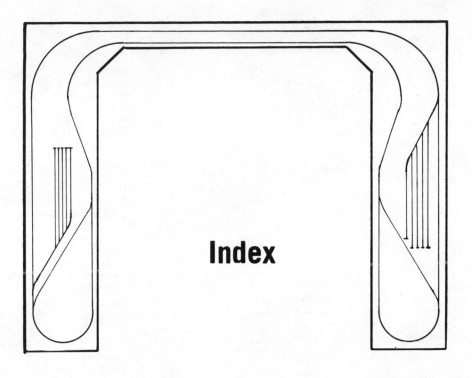

Index

Edited by Steven Bolt